Walk v

The joy of l

John and Pauline Bagg

ISBN 978-1-909694-00-2 (Paperback)

ISBN 978-1-909694-01-9 (ebook)

Published by Syndo Ltd - Linking Passion and Purpose

www.syndo.co.uk

Twitter: @syndoltd

Cover design by Caitlin Bagg (Instagram @cbxgraphics)

For our children,

who have brightened our journey.

CONTENTS

RECOMMENDATIONS

'This is a book for the hungry hearts. The hearts that want to go deeper in life with God. That is, going beyond what we believe, or even say we believe about Him, to what we experience and how we actually live. It's also a book for those who want to understand and grow in discernment. John and Pauline bring the two together as they encourage us to "become more familiar with the ways of God and the Word of God" so that our life is a continual response to His leading. As they write, it's evident these aren't just words on a page but a life they also live. This book is full of gems of truth, both inspirational and practical.'

Susan Sutton, International Director, WEC.

'Contained in this little gem are the secrets of a fruitful life in Christ. Simply put, this book is the most common-sense description of lives devoted to the cause of Christ that I've read. Most of us will never find ourselves at the top of a ladder during a thunderstorm, however if we apply the wisdom contained here, we will find ourselves in the place God has for us and know the joy of abiding with Him.'

Serena McCarthy Urban Saints, UK

ACKNOWLEDGEMENTS

To God, for everything, and for everyone He has given us to be a part of our journey.

To our families, who have loved us, shaped us and nurtured us into adulthood and beyond.

To our children, who journey with us and make the journey so much fun. We love a bit of family banter even if Mum's not always keen!

To those who never gave up on us, even when it seemed most unlikely that we would be able to do the things the Lord called us to; who have stood with us, prayed for us, cheered us on, told us off, and kept us facing in the right direction; who have gone before, and who have given us testimony in written and living form as a witness to the blessings of an obedient life; and who mentored us at crucial stages in our journey.

To the leaders whom we have served and served with. For your examples of tenacity, of courage, of perseverance, of grace, of willingness to keep going, and of willingness to make costly decisions for the sake of the Kingdom.

To our friend, Andrew Bowker, who not only served tirelessly as the Chair of the board of WEC UK during our time in leadership but who went the extra mile by helping us gather our thoughts into something coherent that could work as a book.

And finally, to those who encouraged us in the process of publishing this book. To Glenn Myers, Louis and Susan Sutton and to Serena McCarthy.

Thank you.

FOREWORD

Every generation of God's people is unique. We celebrate that.

What each generation of people has in common is that they must discover what the Lord has planned and prepared for them. Each generation will do things differently to those that have gone before; each will do amazing things, and each will make mistakes. Somehow, through each generation, the Kingdom of God advances and that is beautiful to observe.

To today's generation – it is your time to rise up. Your time to experience the joy of participating in the mission of God and of moving forward in faith to see His Kingdom come. You have the same mandate as every generation that has gone before - to 'seek first the Kingdom'.

In every generation that has gone before there have been men and women of faith who were bright, shining stars whilst others stood back and watched.

To serve or to watch is a choice. It is your choice today. We pray that you will choose wisely – choose to participate.

We hope this book will help you to understand how to do that.

John & Pauline

INTRODUCTION

'Go … surely I am with you always!'

Matthew 28:18-20

Do you ever feel that there is a gaping chasm between what you think a Christian life should be and what you actually experience?

If the answer is 'yes', this book is for you. At the heart of the Christian faith is the message that God came to us, in Jesus, and that through his life, death and resurrection he restored the relationship between God and Man. In this way he made it possible for us to know God as Father. A deep loving, intimate relationship that satisfies the soul and brings meaning and purpose to life.

This is the promise of the Christian faith and yet for so many God still seems distant. Learning to enjoy God's presence as a present, continuous reality, and to know God's heart, His will and His purpose for our lives is primarily a result of having relationship and connection with Him. As such, this kind of experience should be enjoyed by every Christian, not just a select few. It should be our daily reality rather than just a concept to be studied or an abstract theological truth.

Many Christians believe that God speaks and shares His thoughts and feelings with us but are not always sure how He speaks or what He is saying. Perhaps that's you.

Or maybe you have observed others enjoying that type of relationship with God and have longed for it to be your reality.

Our hope is that this book will help to bridge that gap; that it will help you to know how to hear from God for yourself. And not only for yourself – we hope that you will become familiar with hearing from God together with your family, your team, and your church community.

This book is written to build a bridge between aspiration and reality. It contains ideas and practices that will enable you to gain that great treasure; a deep, rich relationship with God.

At its most basic, this book is a love story; our journey with each other and with our God. It tells the story of what we have experienced; what we have learnt along the way; how we get ready for each new stage; and how we try to always be ready whenever He wants to tell us that it's time to get moving again.

We are not telling you our story just so you can say, '*You've had a nice walk!*' The truth is it hasn't always been 'nice'. Sometimes it has been incredibly hard, costly, and sometimes very painful. But He has always been present, so it has always been good. We count it a privilege to have been on our particular journey and we look forward to whatever is next.

The principles and practices that we have learnt, experienced and now share in these pages are based on the convictions we gain from the Bible. We have tried to be as practical as we can and have included other stories to make the material accessible, real and relevant. (In these cases, names have been changed for reasons of anonymity and security.)

Our conviction is that God wants to speak to us. We have had personal experience of Him doing that many times. He has spoken to us individually, and he has spoken to us as a couple, and as a family.

For the last 20 years, we have served together in leadership within a global movement of nearly 2000 people. The people in this movement come from over 50 different nationalities with a shared commitment to '*see Christ known, loved and worshipped among the unreached* peoples of the world*' (*an identifiable people group amongst whom there is no indigenous community of Christians nor adequate resources or commitment to evangelize itself). Within this multi-cultural context, working together, and in partnership with many other church denominations, ministries and Christians around the world, we have had the privilege of seeing God speak to and guide many individuals and groups.

As we have led times of discernment and decision-making, we have witnessed all potential differences evaporate when He speaks. Diversity becomes beautifully united together with one mind and purpose – His heart, His will and His purpose. And this releases faith, conviction, joy, purpose and celebration.

Does that sound appealing?

This is the kind of abundant life that is possible for all Christians. If this is something that you long to experience for yourself, read on.

We write this whilst most of the world is in lockdown because of the COVID-19 pandemic. This will pass, but the world will be changed forever. The ways in which God is leading His people to engage in His Kingdom work will change too – His purpose will remain the same, but His ways of working will be different. In the coming months and years, the effects of this pandemic will continue to ripple around the globe. There will be a fresh emergence of Christians as bearers of hope, joy, grace, mercy and as witnesses to the Good News of salvation in Christ.

For that to happen, we need to be in the right place at the right time. That requires each of us to have a responsive heart. We will need to *walk in the garden with God* (Genesis 3:8). In the walking, there will be much talking, much listening and much learning. If you let Him, He will lead you, guide you, steer you – as an individual, and as part of whatever Christian community you are part of.

We do not know where He will lead you, or what He will say. We do know He will be with you always and that He is trustworthy. Let Him take you where He is going so that you can join in with Him in what He is doing.

Are you up for it?

We hope so, and we hope this book will support you in that desire.

1 WALKING IN THE GARDEN

'My Presence will go with you, and I will give you rest. ... If Your presence does not go with us then do not send us up from here.'

Exodus 33:14-15

Do you believe that 'walking with God' should be our normal, daily experience?

In the encounter between God and His servant Moses in Exodus 33, God promises Moses that His presence would go with him and Moses boldly replies: *'Good – if you're not with us, then please don't make us go anywhere.'*

When God asks us to do something it can make us feel exposed, vulnerable or 'out on a limb'. Moses wanted to make sure that God would be with him and the people of Israel before he set out. He wanted the assurance of the presence of God with them on the journey.

Like Moses, many Christians want this reassurance before they will step out in obedience. They want to do things with God, but they want some extra assurance or proof or experience that God is with them before they do so.

But we live in a different paradigm to Moses. God has promised us that He will always be with us, and He has already come to make His home with us.

What does that mean? It should enable us to move forward with an assurance that Moses did not have.

In the old testament God appeared at 'moments', awesome moments but in moments and in external signs, NOT in an internal, indwelling, continual presence.

In the next verses of Exodus, we read of Moses' 'seeing'

the goodness of God on top of Mount Sinai such that his face became radiant before the people and he had to wear a mask. Elsewhere we read of Elijah's experience on Mount Horeb, as he heard the 'gentle whisper' of God (1 Kings 19:9-18). And we read of the disciples who saw Jesus transfigured on the mountain (Matthew 17 and Mark 6). These were awesome 'mountain top' moments where the glory of the Living God broke into the created order.

But these experiences were not normative or continuous, they were exceptional and momentary.

If we expect or aspire to make them the normative Christian experience, then we create some problems for ourselves and for those we serve. Leaders exhaust themselves cajoling people up the mountain. Whilst those who have not been up the mountain are left feeling inadequate or ill-equipped. They have not had the mountain-top experience and conclude that they are unable to fully engage in what God wants them to do because they have not seen God in this way. This is a self-defeating cycle - meeting after meeting, week after week, leaders exhort people to climb, people try to reach the summit (or give up trying), to experience that wonderful moment where they believe all will be sorted and they will be ready to take on the world.

Therefore, we try to climb, or confess that this week we have not climbed well, or worse that we slid into a valley.

Personally speaking, we became tired of being cajoled in this way, and we want to encourage you that there is a better way.

The perpetual cycle of mountain to valley experience is unhelpful, discouraging and ultimately self-defeating. It led us to the question, *'Why do we try to climb the mountain in the first place?'*

As glorious as it appears, we believe that if you aspire to a mountain-top experience then your aim is far below what you were created and saved to experience. You see, for Moses, Elijah and the disciples, their mountaintop was an 'event'. As awesome as it was, it did not and could not last. It was passing. Moses' radiance faded. Elijah had more work to do, and the disciples immediately fell into a ministry for which they felt ill-equipped and lacked faith. Moses did not see fully, Elijah was not equipped for all he needed, and the disciples did not fully understand.

We believe that we are called to something much more glorious than this.

There is a different reality in the book of Genesis - one which more clearly describes the reality that we were created to experience.

In Genesis chapter 3 we read, '*Then the man and his wife heard the sound of the LORD God as he was walking in the garden in the cool of the day … the LORD God called to the man "where are you"*' (Genesis 5:3-9)?

Was this a one-off walk?

We don't know. We do know that it wasn't presented as a mountain-top 'glory encounter'. Yet God is God, He is glorious. So, the walk with God in the garden must have been a glorious, presence encounter. The text implies that this was a regular event – the difference being that on this specific occasion Adam and Eve had done something they were told not to. They sensed their separation from God and hid themselves from Him.

But surely this is normal - to be expected even. Isn't it? We can't dwell with God as a present continuous reality – can we?

Yes, we can!

We can dwell with Him, as He dwells in us.

God came, in Jesus, to seek and to save those who are

hiding. People like you; people like us. Neither Adam nor Eve, Moses, nor even the disciples at the Transfiguration, had experienced the salvation that is available for us in Christ. For Jesus had not yet died. Just as God promised Moses, *'My presence will go with you'* (Exodus 33:14), Jesus promised the disciples, and us, *'I am with you always'* (Matthew 28:20). His abiding presence with us, in us, always. This is not a 'Passing', this is a 'Presence', a present continuous 'Presence'. The Creator in the created.

We neither aspire, nor encourage others, to seek the 'passing' of a mountain-top encounter. We want to encourage you to live in the 'Presence' of the Living God.

Ask yourself some basic questions:

If God, the Divine Fullness, has promised to be with you always and indwell you by His Spirit, then where are you going to go to find more of Him?

What part of His fullness is missing if He has committed Himself to dwell with you, and be with you forever?

How far we have fallen short if our desire for the deep fellowship and intimate relationship of walking in the garden has been replaced by an unfulfilled longing for mountain-top experiences!

We want to encourage you to 'walk in the garden' with your God. We believe this should be the normal, daily experience for all Christians.

2 ENJOYING THE WALK

'Whether you turn to the right or to the left, your ears will hear a voice behind you, saying, "This is the way, walk in it"'.

Isaiah 30:21

Do you believe that 'walking with God' should be as much (or more) about the journey as it is about the destination?

When John was a child, he used to enjoy going on walks with his grandad. It didn't happen very often but when it did there was always something interesting to learn. For example, he now knows how to enter a hazel coppice (thicket) at the right time of the year, gently tie a knot in a newly growing hazel shoot, and then return to it at a later date to find it has grown into a walking stick with a decent handle. He also learnt how to hold frogs so that you can start a race between them on a fair basis without harming them in the process.

All really important things!

These walks ended where they started; there was no destination to the journey. Simply put, the companionship was the joy. Walking with grandad - copying him, hearing his stories and, all the while, wishing he could wear his grandad's cap. The journey was more important than the destination.

It should be the same in our Christian life. But all too often we live our lives getting ready for what is ahead rather than enjoying the presence of the One we walk alongside. Our eternal reward will be to dwell in His presence. But our present reality is also to dwell in His presence. One day, we will fully know what we now know in part, but there is more than enough for us to know now. If we take time to enjoy the journey and listen to the One who is walking with us, we will learn so much - not just about Him, but also about ourselves and about those around us. God has so much to show and tell us and, through us, to those around.

We once had an experience that helps to illustrate this point.

For seven years we had the privilege of living with our family in Senegal, West Africa. Senegal is a beautiful country full of beautiful people. Having come from the UK the searing heat, the sandstorms, the mosquitoes and the baobab trees took some getting used too!

In Senegal, there are only two seasons: the wet season and the dry season. During the dry season, not only did it not rain, but the heat was dry. The Harmattan wind blew from the Sahara Desert, across West Africa, and into the Gulf of Guinea. It was very much like the experience of being blasted with hot air when you open your oven door to check on the food you are cooking.

The wet season brought rain, was marginally cooler, but extremely humid. When rain was imminent, the sky would darken and turn an eerie shade of crimson; the dark grey clouds would gather ominously overhead, before finally unleashing their load of water amidst the crash of thunder and the power of forked lightning. An awesome experience. At times the lightning would strike a post, a tree or a pylon. And it would do so with ferocity.

On one occasion, John was working at the top of an aluminium ladder when lightning struck a nearby palm tree. The step ladder jumped eight inches in the air, John suffered palpitations and his hair stood on end! The tree died. Thankfully John did not.

Another time, we were lying in bed at midnight and heard

an approaching storm in the distance. We quickly unplugged all our appliances to mitigate against any lightning damage. The lightning struck an electric pylon about fifty metres from our house. All the lights in our house came on and some of the *unplugged* fans suddenly burst into life for a few seconds. Awesome power! The pylon died. Thankfully, we did not!

The pylon was one of the highest points in an otherwise flat landscape, so this was a regular occurrence!

Why did the lightning strike the pylon? Why do we put lightning conductors on tall buildings? Is it because they somehow attract lighting? No, they provide the path of least resistance (and thus protect other structures around). The lightning wants to travel, and it finds the least resistant way to do so.

Why are we telling you this?

We believe that God has a lot of things to say to His people and their communities. Like the pylon, His people should be the path of least resistance. What He wants to say should flow to us and through us. As we live the supernatural life of faith, we should develop the habit of continually and 'naturally' listening to, and sharing, what God is saying.

But this doesn't seem to be the experience of all Christians. How can we grow in this experience?

To begin with we need a conviction.

Before we discuss how to hear from God and know His will, we each have to resolve any doubt that God communicates, that we have the capacity to hear, and that He has things to say to us, individually AND corporately.

Does He speak? Yes!

God is a personal, loving Father who delights in a personal, intimate relationship. He wants to speak, and He wants us to be attentive and to listen. And, at times, He wants us to share what we've heard with others.

If God speaks, then what does He say?

Ultimately that is up to Him! When He speaks, He might speak words of love, affirmation, correction, direction, or encouragement etc. Sometimes there may be periods of silence. (Silent times have their own disciplines and riches which we explore in chapter 8).

For the most part, as we walk with Him, He will have things to say to us.

How amazing is that?

It is all part of walking in the garden together.

3 WALKING WITH PURPOSE

'As a prisoner of God, then, we urge you to live a life worthy of the calling you have received. Be completely humble and gentle; be patient; bearing with one another in love. Make every effort to keep the unity of the spirit through the bond of peace.'

Ephesians 4:1

Did you know that as we walk with God, He works out His purposes in our lives?

We don't want to give the impression that a walk with God is aimless. He is a God of purpose. When we walk with Him, He has purpose – He is accomplishing His purposes in us and through us as we walk where He leads.

In the book of Ephesians, Paul explains some important truths. He tries to help them understand who they are in Christ, and how they have been blessed '*with every spiritual blessing*' (Ephesians 1:3). He explains how they are called, not just out of a life of sin, but into a united Body, His Church. Crucially, he explains that this blessing is for all people, Jews and Gentiles. He then prays that they might understand how amazing all this is, that their knowledge and appreciation of all of this might grow and bear fruit, and that they might all '*be filled to the measure of all the fullness of God' (Ephesians 3:19).*

In chapter 2:21-22 he wrote, '*In [Christ] the whole building is joined together and rises to become a holy temple in the Lord. And in him you too are being built together to become a dwelling in which God lives by his Spirit.*'

These passages of scripture show us that all Christians are called to live a life of unity with each other, a life of fullness and a life of intimacy with Christ.

This is the fullness of life that Jesus also speaks of in John 10:10 - *'I have come that they may have life and have it to the full.'*

This is the fact of our life in Christ. The gift of a full life. Our experience of this full life increases as we walk with God both in terms of our understanding and our personal transformation.

And this growth will be on two basic levels.

There will be personal growth and there will be numerical growth as the number of people participating in this full life increases through the growth of the Church. Person by person.

We each have the opportunity and privilege of participating with Him in exploring what our fullness of life looks like for us whilst simultaneously participating with Him as He brings this full life to others through us.

This is why we are each invited to walk with Him - for what He wants to do in us and what He wants to do through us.

So, when we think of 'calling' (or God's will for our lives) we should not simply think about what He wants us *to do.* It is that, but it is so much more. It is also about who He wants us *to become.*

In the book of Ephesians, Paul also makes it clear that our calling has both an individual and a corporate or collective outworking. We cannot live out our calling on our own. It has to be done within the context of a group of God's people, and within the context of wider society (the people amongst whom God has placed us).

As we walk with God and listen to Him, the things that He says to us will therefore have an inner manifestation, an inter manifestation, and an outer manifestation.

Any Word from God is as much to the whole group as it is to the individuals who make up that group. The whole is much more than the sum of the parts. It is beautiful to see a group of God's people who each know what they are called to do, their unique purpose, and their contribution to the whole group; and to see a group know what they are called to do together. In this way, each person, as part of the whole, will live out their calling in a specific and a general way.

What do we mean by this?

For each individual Christian, our general calling is to increasingly honour God with our lives as part of the Body of Christ - to be salt and light, to understand who we are in Christ, individually and corporately, and to live out Christian, Kingdom values. Our specific calling is the role, the ministry or the task that God has given specifically to us – this is our unique contribution.

How beautiful would it be if all Christians were discipled to expect to hear God's voice as part of their normal daily experience and in answer to their questions in life?

What power would it unleash in the Church if everyone expected to hear and was equipped to discern what God was saying to them?

We long to see every Christian knowing, with deep conviction, that what they are doing is what God has called them to do. Why? Because with this conviction comes increased faith, peace, a capacity to endure trials and deep joy in service.

If we listen to and follow God, He will help us navigate the journey. It's a unique and a personal walk, but it's also a walk together with other people, each of whom are also on their own unique and personal walk.

When John took walks with his grandad, it was rarely just the two of them - siblings and cousins often went along too. As they walked along together, each one had their own personal experience of the journey - some parts related only to themselves, some parts related to the joint activities. But they all enjoyed the walk and got back to the house together, all the richer for having been part of the walk!

4 RECOGNIZING GOD'S VOICE

'Therefore, I urge you, brothers and sisters, in view of God's mercy, to offer your bodies as a living sacrifice, holy and pleasing to God – this is your true and proper worship.'

Romans 12:1

Do you believe that it is possible to hear what God is saying?

Various sources on the internet estimate that the average adult makes 35,000 remotely conscious decisions each day. What shall I eat? What shall I wear? What shall I buy? What do I believe? How should I vote? Who should I meet up with? What job will I get? How should I answer this email? Etc.

We could compile another list of questions that relate to groups: What should we do? What should our priorities be? Who should join with us? What roles should we each have? Who is organising us? When should we meet?

Have you come across people who just seem so connected to God? They seem saturated with the presence of God. They always seem to have a wise word and to hear from Him with ease? They have the gift of being able to differentiate between lots of thoughts, ideas and opinions and find what God wants. We might call these people discerning. Discernment might sound like a mysterious gift obtained by a mystic few. But it is the privilege, and should be the experience, of all of Christians to be able to hear what He is saying, even in amongst all the tweets, soundbites, advice and messages we receive each day.

In Philippians 1:9-10 Paul writes, '*And this is my prayer: that your love may abound more and more in knowledge and depth of insight, so that you may be able to* **discern** *what is best and may be pure and blameless for the day of Christ, filled with the fruit of righteousness that comes through Jesus Christ – to the glory and praise of God.*'

Here the word discern is used to describe the ability to test, to approve, to recognise as genuine.

There are some helpful examples from every-day life that illustrate the principle of discernment. Perhaps you've seen people in the fruit section of your local shop who can tell whether a melon is ripe by tapping the bottom of it and listening for the sound. Or others who think carefully about what they eat and then make good choices about what will be healthy for them. Or others, who scrutinise the ingredients in a product and make sure that there is nothing in it that will be bad for them. In the realm of healthy eating, these are people show discernment.

How does this relate to Christians?

To be spiritually discerning is to determine whether something we hear is from God, from 'the world', from ourselves, or from the enemy (the devil).

To be spiritually discerning is to always choose that which is in line with God's Kingdom principles, His will and His purpose. To be spiritually discerning is to have the capacity to test what we hear (from all the different sources), and to choose what is good, true and noble in every decision.

If we can get this right, we are spiritually discerning.

Some of the decisions we have to make relate to actions and habits of daily life. The Bible gives us clear guidance on many things – so knowing what the Bible says is a good way to discern God's will.

Are you unsure whether to watch a particular film or read

a particular book? Is it good for you (is it edifying, will it build you up)? Will it be helpful for you? If you are unsure, that is probably an indication in itself that it is not good for you. But you can also ask those with greater spiritual maturity whether they would watch the film or read the book.

As we are in a relationship, we can also ask God Himself – He has the capacity to help us make good decisions.

If we think of discernment as being a bit like a muscle, each small decision or small step you take in the right direction will strengthen your discernment muscle. The more you use it, the stronger it will become. This will enable you to increasingly make good decisions.

Some decisions are very difficult, especially ones which go in the opposite direction to what all your friends are doing; or what the prevailing culture of the day would dictate to you. But, even then, when we take time to discern what God is saying, and do it, we will experience His peace. That peace is the evidence that you have discerned God's will in that particular situation.

A walk with God may bring us to the point where we have to make difficult decisions. For example, in our culture we normally encourage our children to aspire to get a good education and training; get a good job; to buy a house and to build a pension for their future security. There is nothing wrong with any of these, but what if God is wanting to lead them on a different path.

We have had to face that challenge. To be obedient and walk with God where He was leading has required us at different times to give up our professions; to sell our house; and to live with less income that we would otherwise have earned. It is not easy to turn away from what everyone else is doing to follow a different path. But it is easier when God has made that path clear to you. And it is easier when He shares His peace with you every time you make a decision that aligns yourself with His purpose. Looking back, we can see some of the material things that we have lost – but we have gained peace and intimacy with Him. And we have seen Him work in and through our lives. Today, we can honestly say that we do not feel any sense of material loss, but even if we could, we would not go back and change any of our decisions because of what we have gained, spiritually.

Becoming increasingly familiar with the character and purposes of God is a crucial part of our walk with Him. It helps us to stay on track and not to become distracted or take a wrong turn. It helps us to stand firm and persevere in our walk even when the terrain gets difficult. It helps us to know what God says. When we know God has spoken, it is a bit like sifting a nugget of gold from a tray of mud as everything else is washed away.

All Christians have the capacity to discern. But in order to grow in this capacity, there are important principles that we must apply.

Firstly, we must understand and acknowledge the source of all godly wisdom. This is the Spirit of God. The Spirit who dwells in all Christians is the Spirit who enables us to discern the voice of God (1 Corinthians 2:14).

Take this to heart.

Wisdom comes from the Spirit, and that same Spirit helps us to discern it. All Christians have the Spirit in them, so all Christians have this capacity. The more we use this capacity the more discernment we can experience.

Secondly, we must walk with God to understand His ways. Perhaps this is difficult to appreciate when we first become a Christian. But over time, this capacity to discern God's voice becomes more familiar, and an increasingly natural part of our walk with God.

To understand His ways, we need to read His Word and

ask Him to speak. You can also observe the lives of those who you consider to be more discerning than you. Over time, as you become more familiar with the ways of God and the Word of God, you will grow in your capacity to discern His voice.

It is like training people to detect forged bank notes. The trainees are not introduced to the infinite number of forgeries. They are trained to become intimately familiar with a real bank note – how it feels, how it looks, how it smells. That way, whenever they come across any forgery, they immediately 'know' that it is different to a real bank note.

Have you ever had that experience?

Someone tells you that God has told them to do this or that, and immediately alarm bells ring inside of your head. You know that God would never say that – it just doesn't stand the test of His character or anything in the Bible. Perhaps, rather than alarm bells, you have a niggling feeling that something isn't quite right or a sense of hesitancy. In either case, it is important to think more deeply about why you feel as you do. This gives God space to speak and for you to discern.

Thirdly, we must have the right motivation. The Apostle Paul makes an interesting connection between love and discernment (Philippians 1:9). If we abound in godly love - a love that honours God, serves others, and denies self - then we will be able to judge or discern His will. We can hold that as a helpful framework for every decision we have to make: Will what I am about to do honour God? Will it help other people? Will it put other people first, before my needs? If the answer to those questions is 'yes', then it will be a good choice. If it is 'no', then think again!

Fourthly, we must be careful not to follow the ways of the culture around us simply because that is what everyone else is doing. If everyone is doing something, that does not necessarily mean that we should. It doesn't necessarily mean that we shouldn't either, but discerning people question what they do and why they do it. Are we shaped primarily by the values of the world in which we live, or by the values of the Kingdom into which we have been called? We need renewing. We are instructed not to conform to the pattern of the world, but to be transformed by the renewing of our minds, then we will be able to test and approve what God's will is – His good, pleasing and perfect will (Romans 12:2).

Finally, we must guard our hearts and our minds – in other words, we must be careful what we allow in. We are exhorted to fill our minds with true, noble, right, pure, lovely, admirable, excellent and praiseworthy things (Philippians 4:8). We are all affected by what goes into our minds. It is all too easy to discount this instruction, because we want to exercise the 'right' we all like to think we have to watch what we want, read what we want, and listen to what we want. But we must remember these choices not only affect our heart and mind; they also affect our capacity to discern the voice of God. That thought should sober us.

We can all grow in our capacity to know the voice of God. This is a journey of deepening intimacy and increasing familiarity with God. And it is a journey of taking responsibility for our actions in order to be in the best place to make the right decisions.

There are no shortcuts here. If you are unfamiliar with discerning the voice of God, then be encouraged that in making some changes to your life, you can increase your capacity to hear Him. On the other hand, if your mind is cluttered, and you don't take steps to unclutter it then do not be surprised if you find discernment a challenge. Anyone that you know to be a discerning person has not become so quickly; it has been a journey of deliberate choices.

Hearing God's voice is not meant to be the privilege of a few; it is a blessing available for all Christians. When making decisions, we can either choose to do it alone, or we can choose to involve God. But why go it alone when you can make decisions together with the One who knows everything – the One who loves you, desires to bless you, to transform you, and to equip you to participate in what He is doing?

It is the invitation of God in the garden.

5 GOD SPEAKS

'God blessed them, and said to them…'

Genesis 1:28

Do you believe that God still speaks today?

Later, we will look in more detail at how God speaks, but let's settle any doubts once and for all that He does speak. It is absolutely crucial that we begin our walk with a conviction that God speaks, and an expectation that He will speak to us. You may not have experienced this, or you may not know how to access the experience. But having this conviction has to be the starting point.

One reason for this, perhaps especially in the West, is that our beliefs tend to be shaped by head knowledge rather than by lived experience. We can have very well formulated theology and doctrine (knowledge about God), but very little intimacy with the One with whom we walk. To try and explain the difference between head knowledge and lived experience, let's take an example from the Psalms.

'The LORD wraps Himself in light as with a garment.' (Psalm 104:2)

The Psalmist has struggled to find words to describe his revelation of who God is. Do you believe that God is clothed in a garment of light? If so, do you believe this because you have experienced a revelation of a God who is wrapped in light, or because you have read the Psalmist's words? It is certainly right to accept things by faith and not just by sight, but let's not allow that approach to rob us of an intimacy that is ours to enjoy. When we do this, we settle for a second-hand experience of God. Where our belief is based on an intellectual assent rather than an experienced reality, we are living impoverished lives.

We live in a different covenant relationship with God than the Psalmist did. Our relationship with God should be more intimate and more personal. For we have a continuous, indwelling Presence that the Psalmist did not have. We are in Christ and He is in us. Therefore, can't our experience of who He is be superior to that of the Psalmist?

Take a step back and reflect on your experience of God, NOT your understanding of God. Describe Him. Have you ever been overwhelmed by His mysteriousness, His awesomeness, His majesty? Do you struggle to put into words your vision of who He is?

The Christian faith is not primarily an intellectual pursuit – it is a relational pursuit – His pursuit of us and our pursuit of Him. The Apostle Paul writes in the book of Philippians, '*I want to know Christ*' (Philippians 3:10), not, 'I want to know Christianity!' It is the pursuit of knowing a Person. Our hope and goal in writing this book is that resting in His presence AND hearing the voice of God might become your ongoing, regular reality. In this way, intimacy with the whole Godhead – Father, Son and Holy Spirit – will be the growing experience of all of us.

How then can we increase our conviction and expectation that God speaks? Let's consider three different types of testimony that bear witness to this truth.

The Word of scripture

From the very first verses of scripture, God has revealed Himself as One who speaks. In the creation account in Genesis, we see the phrase '*And God said*' repeated over and over. God spoke. Then He goes further. In Genesis 1:26 He says, '*Let us make mankind in our image*'. The 'us' is God. This shows that the Trinity of Father, Son and Holy Spirit communicate amongst themselves. If we are made in

His image, it is reasonable to accept that we too are made to communicate; not merely with one another but also with Him, the God who created us. In the verses that follow, we see how God followed through with this divine act of creation. He did exactly as He said He would – '*So God created mankind in his own image, in the image of God he created them; male and female he created them*' (v27). Next, He begins to speak to them (v28) – '*God blessed them and said to them…*'. This is an immediate outworking of the intimate relationship between the Creator and the created. There are two important truths to recognise here that underpin our journey of discernment.

Firstly, God doesn't speak merely because we, His creation, have ears to hear. We are not the cause of God's desire to communicate. He speaks because He wants to. It is in His nature to communicate, and He will do it regardless of our attentiveness.

Secondly, it is an inestimable privilege to have been created with the capacity to hear the voice of the living God, and to be able to participate in conversation with Him. In fact, for some Christians this truth can seem too good to be true. They think, 'Surely God is too awesome and holy to speak to me?' This mindset is a tremendous hindrance and a denial of the very thing that Christ came to accomplish, namely that we might have an intimate relationship with Him – a relationship in which we can talk to one another. His desire to communicate with us is an expression of His nature, and it is a source of great joy to Him when His children seek to listen and obey. If you want to delight God, listen to His voice, let Him speak to you . . . and then do whatever He tells you.

The testimony of people in the pages of scripture

It might be reasonable to conclude that all the examples mentioned above took place before the Fall when sin entered the world and broke the relationship between God and man and that communication is now no longer relevant to us because we have lost that capacity because of the Fall. Or that the traumatic fracture of relationship that took place due to man's rebellion against God has unavoidably affected our capacity to hear and God's desire to talk.

But as we look through the pages of scripture, we don't read that.

In Genesis chapter 3, immediately after the Fall, we read of God's forensic exploration of what had happened and why. Throughout this examination God speaks to His creation – the serpent, the man, and the woman. He declares His just punishment, and He explains what will happen.

Sin and the Fall are not barriers to God's capacity to speak nor our capacity to listen and understand.

Throughout the pages of scripture, we read of character after character who is recorded as having heard the voice of God. Genesis 4:6 – '*The LORD said to Cain…*', Genesis 6:13 – '*So God said to Noah…*', Genesis 12:7 – '*The LORD appeared to Abraham and said …*', Exodus 3:4 – '…*God called to Moses from within the bush…*', Joshua 1:1 – '… *the LORD said to Joshua…*', 1 Samuel 3:4 – '… *the LORD called Samuel* …'. To this list we could add King David, Solomon, the prophets, Mary, Joseph, Elizabeth, Simeon, the Apostle Paul and the elders at Antioch.

God did not speak to them all in the same way. He communicated in whatever way was required for them to understand, and at the time that they needed to hear.

Do not allow yourself to think, for one minute, that this cannot be your experience today. It is the God's delight to speak to you.

The testimony of people throughout Church history

Has God stopped speaking to people?

There are some that believe that all that we ever need to know and understand is contained within the sixty-six books of the Bible, and that God no longer speaks. Personally, we do not hold that conviction. Our reading of Church history, contemporary testimony and personal experience would prevent us from holding that view. Above all else, we believe that this view is inconsistent with the nature of a God who loves to communicate. Pick up any biography of a Christian and you will read of the ways in which God has spoken and led them into action. It never ceases to amaze us the diversity of ways in which God speaks to His children.

We remember a young Asian lady recounting to us how she had sought God for a word regarding her future direction and felt led to pray through *Operation World* (a research and prayer guide to mobilise pray for every nation of the world). She did this faithfully, praying through each country day by day. She simply asked God to show her where in the world He wanted her to serve. She prayed through Afghanistan, Albania … Barbados … China … Denmark … through all the countries listed alphabetically. The year went on … Jordan, Kazakhstan, Laos and on … Peru, Qatar, Rwanda. Day by faithful day she continued in her conviction that God would make it clear. Ukraine, Vietnam and then … Yemen. On that day her heart broke. She wept with a compassion that she had not experienced before, and longed that Christ would be known, loved and worshipped amongst the peoples of that nation.

That day she knew that this was God speaking to her, communicating something of His heart for the people of Yemen. So, she went to love and serve them, to be the channel through whom God wanted to love and serve them.

6 GOD SPEAKS TO ME

'He said to me, "Son of man, stand up on your feet and I will speak to you". As he spoke, the Spirit came into me and raised me to my feet, and I heard him speaking to me.'

Ezekiel 2:1-2

Do you know with certainty that what you are currently doing is God's will for you?

In the book of James, we read of the instability that comes from being double-minded, which leads to doubt (James 1:8). Contrast this with the delight of having an 'undivided heart' which brings a clarity to life, purpose, devotion and awe of God (Psalm 86:11).

We do not exist in some wonderfully isolated bubble, free from influence. We never do. We are being influenced all the time. God speaks, but He is not the only voice in our lives. The key question is *who has the loudest voice in our life?*

Is it the One who knows all things? The One who loves you deeply?

If it is not God that we are listening to, then who is it?

Someone, or something, is speaking into our hearts, lives and minds to shape our values, convictions and actions all the time.

Is it the world – media, politics, materialism, culture?

Is it the enemy (the devil) – he always speaks things that will draw you away from living the way God wants you to?

Or is it the expectations of others?

Ezekiel was a prophet. He spoke forth the word of God. That was his calling and that was what God equipped him to do. The call to Ezekiel was to ready himself - '*stand up on your feet and I will speak to you*' (Ezekiel 2:1).

In the same way, God speaks to us. We are all called to speak forth the word of God to our communities. But are we ready to receive what God has to say to us?

The next time you are in a group with other Christians you might like to try this. Ask the group the following questions one at a time. Ask them to raise their hands if they believe that:

God has a plan and a purpose.

God has a global plan.

God has a plan for the group.

God has a plan for each member of the group.

We have done this, and it is our experience that most Christians will raise their hands in response to each of those statements.

Somehow, we all have a belief that God has a plan! This is a good place to start. (You might want to then ask them to explain why they think that.)

Next, with the same group, ask them to raise their hands if they know:

What is the purpose for this group?

What is the purpose for them as individuals?

It is our experience that most hands will NOT be raised.

This is sad for many reasons.

It highlights a functional disconnect between what we believe and what we experience. This dichotomy creates instability and fragility. We can share a general conviction publicly, but internally we can be conflicted. Perhaps worse, we begin to think that whilst it might be true for others it cannot be true for me, and that therefore God must somehow love me less than others. Or that clarity from God is the privilege of a few holy, special people.

What is even more dangerous is that this instability, fragility, and uncertainty is being multiplied throughout the Body of Christ.

If this is your experience, we hope that as you work through this chapter, you can move the short but significant distance between being convinced that God speaks and the expectation that He wants to speak to YOU!

The way to do this is for each one of us to take responsibility for ourselves, and to ask God to lead us into a place of clarity, conviction and certainty, such that the gap between conviction and experience is closed.

In many cases, Christians feel stuck; not because they are unwilling to do something, but rather because they don't know what that 'something' should be, and because they are inexperienced in the discernment process.

This leads to a lack of faith and confidence in prayer. Not because we don't believe God can do all things but because we are either not sure how to pray, or we are not praying with any sense of conviction. And when we don't know what we are called to or are not sure what God is saying about a matter, we are open to deception and manipulation. This deception can come from one of two directions.

Firstly, from the enemy. We see an example of this in the account of the Fall in the garden of Eden. The serpent was very subtle. He did not give Eve a completely different command to the one God had given her; rather, he sought to undermine her conviction about what God had said to her - '*Did God really say …*' (Genesis 3:1)? In the same way, we are susceptible to being separated from the things God has told us to the degree that we then lack conviction. How much more will we be led astray if we do not know what He has said in the first place?

Secondly, it can come from people around us. Some may deliberately wish to deceive us, but others may simply be well-meaning, strong, and passionate with their own opinions. Their strength of feeling or passion can inadvertently sway you into doing something that God has no intention for you to do. Being discerning and knowing what God is saying releases in us the power and certainty to say 'No' as well as 'Yes'!

We are convinced that all Christians should have confidence in His calling, whatever that might be – this is absolutely critical to being steadfast and faithful.

We have had, and continue to have, the privilege of serving in a mission context. One of the characteristics that is common to all the people that we serve alongside is a very strong sense of calling.

At the same time, we have always been part of a local church context and have Christian friends working in many other spheres of life who equally have a very strong sense of calling to what they are doing e.g., in church ministry, in business, in teaching, in nursing etc. But those with a strong sense of calling and conviction make up a much smaller percentage of the whole Church. There are far too few Christians who have this strong sense of conviction.

This means that a sense of calling is often seen as the preserve of a small portion of God's Church - by practice though NOT by design.

More tragically, it indicates that there is a level of intimacy with God that has been made possible in Christ, that is not being experienced by all Christians. It is as though, despite the invitation to walk and journey with God, many are choosing to ignore the invitation or content themselves to sit and watch.

Pauline loves watching tennis. Imagine her excitement if someone told her that they had centre court tickets for her to watch the finals of the All-England Lawn Tennis Championships at Wimbledon. It would be strange if she were to accept the ticket, drive to the 'Home of English Tennis' and then sit in the car park to listen to the game, hearing the roar of the crowds from outside the grounds!

Let's each be people who fully accept God's invitation to walk with Him – to hear what He says and to follow where He leads.

As God speaks, let His voice be the loudest voice in your life.

7 GOD SPEAKS TO US

> *'(Christ) is before all things, and in him all things hold together. And he is the head of the body, the church; he is the beginning and the firstborn from among the dead, so that in everything he might have the supremacy.'*
>
> Colossians 1:17-18

Do you believe that a group of people can discern what God wants to say to them as a group?

Imagine if everyone in the whole global Church believed that God speaks and daily heard from Him. Wow … that would be amazing!

But being a sensitive, listening people is not meant to be a blessing just for us as individuals. It is meant to be an experience enjoyed together as well.

The Apostle Paul frequently compared the church to a body and to a family. In both metaphors he is trying to help us to understand that we are so much more than a collection of individuals. We are, in Christ, bound together.

If this is true, then it also follows that the discovery of our calling is more than a personal journey; it is a collective one. The call of God should be discerned personally, but it should also be discerned collectively. There is little place within the Body of Christ for an independent spirit. In fact, the call of God only ever works itself out with genuine beauty and winsomeness within the context of the Body - all together, all dependent together on Christ the Head.

Unless this is being worked out, there is always the risk of division, hurt, pride, angst and deception. Sadly, all of this has been and continues to be prevalent in the Church and in missionary endeavours. In His grace, God is still able to work through such a fractured and fragmented Body, but we are convinced that there is a better way.

We know that we cannot solve all the ills of the Church. God can and will do that.

But we can each take responsibility to adapt our practices to better reflect the way God intends us to live and serve together. We will be all the better for it, and the work of our hands will be all the more fruitful for it.

This kind of collective discernment can be a real challenge, especially for those of us who have been brought up with the conviction that independence is good, that it is a mark of strength, and that it should be commended.

This is a lie, and it damages people, society, and the Church. It is the enemy's attempt to fragment the Body of Christ.

It is hard to think of any decision that only affects one of us and no-one else. Lives are never lived in isolated bubbles. Rather, we live with interconnected relationships, where the decisions and actions of one can affect many others.

Even if we seek input from God and others, it might still be individual decision-making – I have a decision to make, I seek direction from God, I seek counsel from people around, and then I make a decision.

But what does it mean for a group of people to work together to discern God's will for them as a group? This group may be a ministry team, a whole church, or a global mission agency. Or it might be a family or a couple. In other words, any situation where there is more than one person making decisions about what they should do.

In group decision-making, God's purposes are not worked out merely by the contribution of numerous individuals. Yes, we are individuals, but we are also part of the Body of Christ. In this Body, each part has a contribution to make individually to the whole group. The collective outcomes are much more than the sum of our individual contributions. Therefore, it follows that if we can discern individually, then we can extend that practice and discern corporately.

The Apostle Paul exhorted us to, '*live a life worthy of the calling you have received*' (Ephesians 4:1). As we stated in Chapter 3, our conviction is that this calling has a personal AND a corporate expression.

When we apply the principles of listening and hearing the voice of God to the group dynamic, the fruit is multiplied. The basic principle is that a group of people, with a wide diversity of spiritual maturity, experience, age, gifts, culture, language, passions, and convictions, can find unity in Christ and in His purposes for them as a group. This experience is a truly beautiful and miraculous thing to witness.

Consider Paul's words in his letters to the Ephesians (4:1-16) and to the Corinthians (1 Corinthians 12:1-31). In these passages, there are some quite remarkable truths that have significance for finding God's will together as a group.

We are united. We are united together in Christ into one Body, and we are united together under one Head. The Body of Christ is not a multi-headed creature. Rather, with Christ at the Head, the Body is knitted together to function together with a united purpose.

As we look at the global Church, we can see all the divisions that have happened through the course of Church history at personal, family, church, and denominational levels – and these divisions continue to this day. Much of this division is founded upon a weak understanding of the unifying power of the Gospel to overcome and reconcile every division to bring unity under Christ. Some of the division represents an unwillingness to take the truth of who we are and make it the reality of how we live. We allow our differences to be a greater reality than our unity in Christ.

These differences might be our cultural bias or our particular theological or doctrinal emphasis on a secondary issue or our denominational practice. But our unity in Christ is, and should be, more important and more precious than anything that might divide us.

This type of radical unity has the capacity to bring all our diversity together under one Head. More than that, it will unite us in a manner which magnifies and celebrates our diversity, rather than trying to minimise it through repressive conformity or endless division. This takes love, grace, truth and mercy, and we have these in abundance through the power of the Holy Spirit within each of us individually, and within us corporately as the Body of Christ.

We are diverse. The Body of Christ is made up of people who think differently, and who have different experiences, convictions, passions and hopes. We are all at different stages in life, and we are all at different levels of spiritual maturity. Beyond that we are also each uniquely gifted and have a unique perspective and contribution to make to any process of group discernment. We must recognise that all this diversity comes from God.

This fact should lead us to serve one another with humility and not arrogance; and we should consider others better than ourselves.

At the same time, we should be content with our gifting, rather than wishing we were someone else. If we can value who we are AND accept that others are a gift to us, then we will go a long way to building unity and discerning God's purpose for any group we are part of.

We are dependent. We are dependent on Christ and the enabling of the Holy Spirit. In humility, we should come to Him to acknowledge that He is the Way, the Truth and the Life. Apart from Him we can do nothing, and so why would we even bother to try? Our best human-empowered efforts are nothing, and our most simple Christ-dependent efforts are everything.

We serve a God for whom nothing is impossible. Why would we try to do anything in our own strength and wisdom? That leads to impoverishment. Weakened by this fundamental misunderstanding of who we are in Christ, we can be unwilling to step out in faith because it all seems too much for us.

We are interdependent. We are all dependent on Christ, and we are all dependent on one another. We are interdependent. This does not mean that we should simply tolerate one another when we have to, but rather we should foster a genuine conviction that 'I cannot do this on my own and I need my brothers and sisters'. This dynamic should not only work itself out amongst the members of any particular local church, but also between local churches within a geographical locality whether that be at local, national or global level.

We are responsible. Each member of the Church has a contribution to make. That is how the Church has been created to function. We are responsible for one another and for our continued participation. For the Body to function, we cannot opt out or let ourselves be passengers or spectators.

One of the leaders of a church we were part of was asked how large his church was. He answered by saying, 'We are a church of 300 going on 60'. What he meant by this was that 20% of the church did 80% of the activity and ministry of the church.

This is not the picture of the Church that Paul paints in his letters in the New Testament. In these letters, we see groups of people who participate together, pull together, and serve together. Not in some homogenous greyness, but in a beautifully united, colourful, diverse array of people. We all have a part to play. The Spirit can speak through any member of the Body of Christ. This is our privilege, but this is also our responsibility. Wisdom is both knowing what to say AND when to say it; it is also sharing what we feel that the Spirit is saying, and doing so with humility, submitting it for the group to test.

We are guided. The Spirit gives gifts and ministries to each of us. He does this for a reason - that we might understand what God requires of us, and that we might be equipped to achieve the task. This participation might be direct - something for me to support and engage with myself. Or it might be indirect - something that I affirm as being for 'us' (the group), but that is for someone else to do. Nonetheless, my affirmation releases me to own it as 'ours', and to participate in praying for that person or ministry with faith and conviction. Ultimately, all that we do in response to God's leading will be for the growth of the Kingdom. That is our privilege.

As we look across the globe today, more people are responding to the Gospel and putting their trust in God than at any other time in the history of the Church. This is making the Church more diverse, and the scope of its activities broader and more varied.

Into this wonderful mosaic of people and activities God speaks, leads and guides all things towards a glorious end. He orchestrates all our activity in a way that is well beyond the capacity of the most gifted and strategic thinkers amongst us. We should never think we can control what He is doing; we can't. But we can seek Him together to participate in what He is doing, both individually, but even more so with the group of people among whom He has placed us – our family, our team, our church.

In addition, with this explosion of diversity in the global Church, there has never been a time when the need to reflect on what it means to seek the mind of God together is more greatly needed. The traditional, Western-style patterns of doing this that have dominated multi-cultural groups for so long simply won't work. They won't work in the cultures where the Church has emerged in recent decades, and they will be increasingly ineffective in traditionally Christian countries where the Body of Christ is becoming more culturally diverse.

Let's be open to what God is doing, and let's find ways that celebrate and facilitate this diversity. Participation in group discernment is one way of doing this. It is crucial.

Through this approach, Christ will shape the Church of the future, because He is the Head of the Church.

Christians should be a united, diverse, dependent, interdependent, responsible and guided Body of people. It is to this body of people that God has things to say, things to show and instructions to give.

If you're not sure what He is calling you to then keep reading. Equip yourself to find out and then join in with what He is doing!

Later, we will look at how God might speak to us, but at this point we want you to move forward with these three convictions:

God speaks!

He wants to speak to us!

He knows how to speak in a way that we can understand.

8 WHEN THERE IS SILENCE

'O my God, I cry by day, but you do not answer, by night, but I find no rest.'

Psalm 22:2

Do you experience times when you are seeking God, but He seems silent?

We believe that God wants to communicate all the time. But we also know that there are seasons when we don't hear Him. Before we reflect on some possible reasons for this, we want to clearly state one thing:

We must NOT confuse silence with absence.

When God is silent, He is still with us. His indwelling presence is a promised, continual reality, even when we cannot hear His voice. This is a great consolation and foundation to rest.

There are a number of possible reasons for times of silence, and we're going to look at four. There are more, but if you start with these whenever you are experience a time of silence from God, then you will be in a good place for Him to lead you to other reasons.

If you wish to gain deeper intimacy with God and hear what He is trying to communicate with you, try to identify which one relates most closely to your current circumstance, and then apply the action to move forward.

1: God is speaking, but we are not listening.

There are many reasons why we may not be listening. For example, we might not want to know what God has to say. We might be fearful of what He might say. We might think that we know the answer ourselves. We might think that God is not interested in our questions, or that we are too insignificant for God to be bothered with. Any of these will have the effect of stopping up our ears.

We have lost count of the number of people who have shared with us that they don't want to listen to what God might be telling them in case He tells them to go somewhere or do something difficult.

Pauline has had that experience personally.

After returning from living in Senegal for 2 years, we spent a year at Bible college in Norwich. As we came to the end of that year, all the students were talking and praying about what they were going to be doing next. I knew that we should pray about this and ask God to show us, but I was too scared to in case He asked us to return to Senegal. So, I didn't. I avoided praying about it. I deliberately didn't give God any opportunity to speak to me about it.

I kept this up for weeks, but it became increasingly unsustainable. Partly because we were regularly asked, 'What next?' But mainly because taking this position was completely at odds with what I knew life as a disciple of Jesus should be like. I couldn't on the one hand call Jesus 'Lord' and on the other hand completely shut Him out. The two positions were untenable and wrong.

Eventually God made this clear to me. I repented of my wrong behaviour and asked Him what He wanted us to do next – now I was open to listen! As soon as I took this difficult step, I was able to hear what He was saying.

I learnt two valuable lessons through that experience. Firstly, I can't hear what God wants to tell me if I'm deliberately not listening. Secondly, by not listening I was robbing myself of the privilege of hearing God speak to me.

Action: Please hear this – God loves you and cares for you. His plans and purposes are the doorway to much rich blessing. It's madness to not listen to whatever He has to say. The route back from not listening is simply to confess, seek forgiveness, and start again. You can unstop your ears with a change of heart. God will always be waiting.

Coming to God conditionally is problematic. Setting conditions effectively acts as a filter. It is like coming to a waterfall to fill a large jar, and then taping a straw to the mouth of the vessel before trying to fill it. Rip away the straw! Throw the whole vessel under the waterfall and it will fill quickly. In the same way, throw away your fears, your conditions. Tell God that you want to be open and ask for His help to be open. This might be a tremendous act of courageous faith. Your steps towards doing this might feel like weak, faltering ones. But in doing so you will find new levels of freedom in Christ.

We are not called to be people who live risk-free, comfortable lives. It is clear from Jesus' teaching that we are called to be disciples, to pick up our cross, to follow Him, and to seek first the Kingdom of God. This is not simply a concept to be discussed theoretically. It is to be a daily reality in our lives lived for Christ. He speaks, we hear, we follow – wherever He might take us. And as we follow in obedience, He speaks words of encouragement, direction and correction.

This is the life we are called to. This intimacy and discipleship are what Adam and Eve experienced in the coolness of the garden.

2: God is speaking, but we can't hear.

It might be that there is a blockage that deafens us to His voice. This situation should be embraced as a process to work through, rather than a discouragement to cause us to walk away or give up.

Action: Don't allow yourself to simply conclude that God has nothing to say whenever you cannot hear from Him. Take the harder route and to allow the Holy Spirit to search your heart. Perhaps there is some aspect of your life that God wants to bring to your attention, or something that He wants to work on. Perhaps there is some broken relationship that He wants you to restore (or at least do whatever is in you power to do to open the door for restoration to take place). This is not navel gazing or introspection; it is allowing the Holy Spirit to work within you. Use the silence wisely.

Once, we were part of a team that was earnestly praying for some guidance about what to do next. As a team we had several choices before us, and yet we could not find a sense of united conviction about the future. Eventually, it became clear that before we could move forward there were some attitudinal changes that had to take place within the team. So, one evening, rather than spend more time in prayer asking for God's guidance about the matter, we spent time in confession and taking communion together.

This precious moment was like a cork coming out of a bottle. It put the team in the right place, a God-honouring group of united individuals, ready to receive what God had to say. Soon after that, the direction came, and the whole team were mobilised to fulfil what God said. What followed was another part of our journey of faith, and of seeing God perform some amazing miracles of timing and provision. And, importantly, we became a united team of people who loved, encouraged and spurred one another on in the pursuit of God's purpose for us.

3: God is speaking, we have heard but we are choosing to ignore Him.

Listening, hearing and doing must work together. If we listen and hear but don't do, then we might as well not listen in the first place. If there is great blessing and privilege in listening to and obeying God, then conversely there are tragic consequences for not doing so. If intimacy with the Living God is the treasure that we gain from listening, hearing and obeying, then anything less is impoverishment.

It makes no sense to choose to lead an impoverished life, does it? But so many do, whether directly by their actions or indirectly by their inaction. When we make any choice in life, we are also determining to receive the consequences of that choice. If we choose disobedience, then this leads to a deeply impoverished life. Why would we deliberately choose that?

If hearing the voice of God is an expression of intimacy and a source of wisdom, counsel, and guidance; if it delights God to speak; and if He is pleased when His people are open and receptive to His voice; then what is the consequence of not hearing His voice?

The prophet Amos gives us a stark warning. In chapter 8 verses 11-12 we read that due to their rebellion and disobedience, God sent the people of Israel a famine – '*not of food or water but of hearing the words of God.*' The tragic consequences of hearing and not obeying the word of God were weakness and impoverishment. Why would anyone choose this? And yet, in our day just as in theirs, so many of us make this choice time and time again. We are too busy solving all our problems with our own wisdom that we are not applying the God revealed solutions. That, in His words, leads us to needless spiritual impoverishment, even though we HAVE the Word.

Alternatively, rather than ignoring what God says, we can choose to receive it, even if we are doing so in weakness and trembling. When we genuinely seek God, He will work to transform our heart in such a way that we are ready to receive what He says and respond. If we want to grow closer to God, it is imperative that we are willing to walk that journey. This is a tough choice at times.

On a number of occasions, we have listened to people share what they believed God was saying to them, but who subsequently concluded that what He was asking was too difficult and that they were not willing to pursue it further.

If we ever recognise this reaction in our hearts, rather than try to rationalise it and explain it away, we must confront it and call it what it is – disobedience. There is a disobedience of commission (doing what you should not do), and a disobedience of omission (not doing what you should do). Both lead to a barren place, but this doesn't need to be the destination.

Action: The great mercy and grace of God enable us to confess our mistakes and wrong attitudes and find a way through to restoration and release. Let us open our hearts and minds primarily to what God is saying – trusting that His plans and purposes for us are always good even if they are hard.

4: There is silence because God is not speaking.

There are seasons when we do not hear because God is deliberately silent. Silence can be very arresting.

In our marriage, conversation is easy – we can speak freely, and we are also free not to speak. But there are times when a peculiar silence speaks much louder than words. These silences are a 'loud' sign that we need to pay attention to. If we want to maintain a good relationship with each other, we can't afford to simply shrug off these kinds of silences and think, 'It's okay, one day we will speak again.' We need to recognise the silence and explore why it exists – 'Have we done something we shouldn't? Have we not done something we should? Have we forgotten something? Is something wrong?

In the same way, times of silence from God should not be dismissed; they can be deeply significant if we take the time to explore them with Him. We need to consider what this silence might communicate.

Having said that God always wants to communicate, sometimes the thing that God wants to share with us is silence. Just because we seek Him, does not mean that He must speak. Silence is a means by which He can cause us to draw nearer, seek harder, and ultimately become more intimate with Him. If we come to Him expecting that He must speak simply because we are waiting, then silence can be incredibly discouraging. This also demonstrates great arrogance on our part. Silence may be the way in which God leads us into a season when He wants us to dig deeper. It's like a child chasing a retreating wave and only realizing how deeply they have gone when they find themselves overwhelmed by the returning wave. In the silence, God takes us deeper.

Action: If we find ourselves in a place of silence, and we have eliminated the possibility that there is a blockage and that our hearts are in the right, then the only thing we can do is wait. But wait patiently and expectantly. Wait proactively. The process of listening, and in this case waiting, is as important as anything that God says to us. And it's not a passive state of being. Waiting well is the space in which God, by His silence, causes us to reflect more deeply on questions of faith and relationship, personal transformation and holiness, character, and conviction. Silence causes us to notice what is really in our hearts.

So, wait. Prayerfully. You might also like to introduce a time of fasting as a spiritual discipline - going without something in order to express your hunger for more of God.

Don't try and rush ahead. Be content with silence and avoid the temptation to fill the space with your own thoughts and wisdom.

The natural response to times of silence is to cry out to God, 'Where are you?' Perhaps a more helpful question is to sit in the silence and ask, 'Where am I?' Sit with all your thoughts, emotions and feelings in the presence of God and wait. It is NOT a passive, unproductive time – it is space for God to work and show you just what you need to hear as He works in you.

In an age where we are constantly connected and fill every waking moment with something, space and silence can be strange, uncomfortable, and even terrifying. Learning to wait well, is a reward in and of itself.

In the book of Habakkuk, we have a wonderful example of waiting where the prophet had to learn this discipline. Twice he complained to God that He was not listening, that He was not answering, and that He should pay attention to Habakkuk's appeal for an answer.

How often have you felt like that?

But here is that important truth again. Just because you are asking does not mean that God has to say anything. So how can we find peace in that?

Look at Habakkuk – when God finally answered the prophet, He gave him some advice that is still relevant to us all: '*For the revelation awaits an appointed time; it speaks of the end and will not prove false. Though it lingers, wait for it; it will certainly come and not delay*' (Habakkuk 2:3).

Relating this specifically to discernment, we can see that both the *timing* of the revelation AND the *fulfilment* of that revelation are in God's hands. His will and His timing are perfect. This truth releases us to be able to wait in peace. If we can't, two things will likely happen.

Firstly, we will run ahead and fill the gaps with our own thoughts and desires. Even our very best thoughts will never be sufficient to replace God's.

Secondly, we will try and work it out in our own strength and with our own resources. This is exhausting and fruitless. Being discerning enough to know BOTH the timing of His revelation AND the timing of the outworking of it is a precious thing.

John was once mentoring a young man called Chris who wanted to hear some word of direction from God. He had spent two years in Africa and was coming to the end of his time there, and was earnestly seeking God, to know what He should do with the next season of his life.

As the days and weeks passed and the deadline of his return to the UK loomed ever closer, he lost all sense of peace. God was not telling him, and he could not understand why. Whenever they met, they discussed this topic. Over time, Chris began to notice a question in his mind, 'Do I trust God?' As time went on, the conversation slowly evolved. It changed from being focussed on hearing God's direction, towards being about learning to trust God more deeply.

Eventually Chris managed to find a place of peace and trust in which he could wait. In due course, at just the right time, God made it clear to him what to do next. Of course God did – He always does! Learning to wait well is a key discipleship lesson. In the waiting, God changes us.

Always remember that He is God. Whilst He delights to speak with us, to share His heart, His plans and His purpose with us, and to engage us in what He is doing, He is God. He is omnipotent, omnipresent, omniscient, awesome, holy, just, loving, and totally beyond our comprehension. He is different from us. He is our Creator and Sustainer. We are the created and the sustained. He reveals Himself and His plans to us, and He is higher than us. His plans are beyond our understanding until He gives us revelation.

Considering this, our best approach should always be to wait expectantly and more importantly, to walk with humility.

We close this section with a reminder, and a challenge.

Hearing is inextricably linked to our relationship with Him, and to the attitude of our heart towards Him. It is like a treasure hunt, where Christ (and His will) is the treasure. It is a process that should release you to serve God with a strong conviction that you're doing what He has asked you to do and bring you into ever deeper levels of intimacy with Him. The more you engage with Him, the more it will become natural for you to hear Him speak to you.

9 STARTING TO WALK

'Trust in the Lord with all your heart and lean not on your own understanding; in all your ways submit to him and he will make your paths straight.'

Proverbs 3:5-6

Do you want to start the journey of discernment?

We all have to start our Christian journey somewhere.

Every testimony is a wonderful example of God's grace reaching into a person's life and speaking enough truth so they can understand and respond to the offer of salvation in Christ. Every beginning is amazing. In the same way, we each need to start our journey of discernment somewhere.

John's journey started like this:

I became a Christian whilst I was studying Engineering at University in Bristol. For me, coming to faith was a profound experience of 'meeting Jesus'. My world turned from black and white into colour, or put another way, it went from a 2D to a 3D experience. I had no Christian upbringing, and had not attended church regularly whilst growing up, so salvation was a dynamic new experience for me. I was especially struck by the promise of Jesus, 'I have come that they may have life, and have it to the full.' John 10:10 [NIV]. The word 'may' really focussed my thoughts. I understood 'may' to mean that there might be the option that I 'may not' have life to the full. As a new Christian, I looked around the churches I visited, and I could differentiate between those people who chose to have 'life to the full' and those who seemed to have chosen not to! I was eager to choose this fullness of life that was mine in Christ.

The first eighteen months of new life were 'interesting'. I carried on doing the degree course I had started. I began to attend a church, joined a mid-week discipleship group, and started copying what other

Christians did. It quickly appeared to me that this 'fullness of life' meant attending lots of meetings … and I became a little disappointed. There must be more to it than that … surely?! Having not grown up within a local church, I didn't really know what Christians were supposed to do. I began asking the people around me, and I received some advice, some strange looks, and several silent, embarrassed stares before some pressing business seemed to grab their attention in another part of the room! Eventually, my father-in-law gave me some very sound and profound counsel – 'Read your Bible regularly, pray regularly, serve in a church, and do whatever you feel God is telling you'. 'Attend meetings' did not make the list … so I was keen to follow this advice!

This gave me an expectation that fullness of life is primarily worked out through an intimate relationship and dialogue with God and in serving together with other people. God will speak; I can hear from Him. We can hear from Him and we can work together.

It was at this time that I began the habit of journaling; writing down thoughts, verses of scripture, words, prayers … whatever struck me each time I spent time with God, or as I went through the course of the day. I have continued this practice ever since. I record hopes, things I notice, disappointments, fears, blessings, challenges. This has become a huge source of encouragement to me. As I look through these journals going back over the years, I have a record of my conversation in walking in the garden with God.'

Pauline's journey started like this:

I had the privilege of growing up in a Christian home. From as early as I can remember, I heard about Jesus, had the Christian life modelled to me by my parents, and was surrounded by people who prayed for me. It was very natural for me then, at the age of seven, to want to invite Jesus into my life. I remember my dad helping me do that by praying a simple prayer with me one bedtime.

As I grew older, my faith went through some ups and downs. I continued to be mentored by those around me – my parents, my church leaders, my Sunday school teachers, my youth group leaders, my Christian friends, and other Christian family members. But I also began to be distracted by other things, and this affected my priorities. And as soon as other things took priority, I began to make poor decisions.

For a long time, I lived a dual, hypocritical life. On the one hand, I was going through the motions as a Christian (going to church, saying all the right things, etc.), but on the other hand, living a lifestyle that did not in any way honour God.

This dual lifestyle continued after I went to university, but eventually things came to a crossroads after I had been going out with John for a while. One day, I realised that this hypocritical life had to stop. Looking back, I now recognise that this thought was God nudging me.

I decided that I had to either commit my life fully to God, or fully deny Him. Walking with one foot in each camp had no integrity and was becoming increasingly untenable.

So, I asked myself, 'Can I fully deny God's existence?' As I thought about it, the answer was not difficult to find. I only had to look at creation, with all its beauty and complexity, to know without doubt that there had to be a God. As Isaac Newton once said, 'In the absence of any other proof, the thumb alone would convince me of God's existence.'

The physical world around me could not have happened by chance. To believe that required much more faith than believing that there was a Designer. And I knew that that Designer had to be God.

Having settled that I couldn't deny His existence, I knew that I had to fully commit to God, and to live as He wanted. I knew that this would mean making some changes in my life. Again, I can now recognise that this was God's Spirit nudging me. He didn't force His way back into my life, but gently reminded me of His presence. He was patient, waiting for me to give Him my attention again.

I began by recommitting my life to Him and giving Him Lordship over every area of it again. This was a costly decision, because I knew that it would mean ending my relationship with John. At this point, he was not a Christian, and as such I knew that our relationship had no future; our priorities and values from this point on would be too different and incompatible.

When I broke the news to him, he tried to convince me that he was a Christian. He believed that being brought up in a Christian country meant that he was automatically a Christian. Eventually, after some long and interesting debates, he decided that he'd like to go to church with me one Sunday evening. And it was on that occasion that he first heard the Gospel and invited Jesus into his life. Our romance was back on, but this time with God at the centre!

What began as two individual journeys combined together when we got married in 1990. From then on God had the task of leading us together and we had to learn what it meant to be led not as two individuals but as one couple.

In 1991 we were coming to the end of the final year of our university courses, which was also the end of our first year of married life! As we approached the end of the year, John was struck by a verse he read - 'Wake up sleeper, rise from the dead, and Christ will shine on you.' (Ephesians 5:14). We thought about this verse, and we both felt that it was a challenge to us personally to 'rise up' from the path we were on, so that we would find something, an unexpected blessing. 'Yes please!' we, in our innocence, declared to God!

About a year earlier, whilst John had been studying as an engineer in Bristol, he had worked with a company on an office development in Oxford. One of the other engineers was a Christian. This man was from New Zealand and had been in the UK for the previous four years. He came to work one morning to inform the team that he had just heard that he had not been granted an extension to his work visa, and so he would have to return to New Zealand within the next seven days. The following day, he came into the office and offered John a big box which contained a number of different items – magazines, leaflets, flyers, cups, and pencils; all things he had collected from numerous Christian festivals, conferences and other activities whilst in the UK. John had been a Christian for about a year at this point, so he thought that there might be something useful in the box so took it home.

He never investigated what was in the box.

The following summer we got married, found our new home as a married couple, and moved all our worldly possessions into a small one-bedroomed flat. This somehow included the box of 'stuff' from John's engineer friend – still unsorted and unread.

As we approached the end of our final year at university, the company which had been sponsoring John throughout his last year of study wrote to explain that due to the current recession in the UK at the time, the training budget had been cut, and they would not be able to offer him the job after his graduation as they had intended. At the same time, Pauline was having no success in finding a teaching post, despite having excellent references. Her tutor could not explain why she was not getting anywhere. We began to question what was next.

One night, John had a very vivid dream.

In his dream we were both stood under a signpost at a crossroads. To the right we could go and work in Bath – a very beautiful city near to Bristol, and a place that we would have been very happy to settle down in. To the left we could go and work in Belfast. Subsequently, we have visited Belfast many times and found the people of Northern Ireland to be very hospitable and generous. At the time though, our only experience of Belfast was the news reports of the troubles that were ongoing. In that context, Belfast did not seem to be a very inviting prospect. Looking straight ahead the signpost pointed to Burkina Faso.

We knew nothing about the country, and in the dream, John saw a red, dry, barren landscape. But as he looked more closely, he saw that this was where there was joy. In the dream, this was the road we chose to take.

We carried on thinking about what to do after we graduated. The weeks passed. We came to the end of our degree courses, and the contract on our flat was about to run out. We decided to pack up and relocate to stay with Pauline's parents for the next few weeks whilst we decided our next steps.

As we were packing up, we found 'the box' under the bed and had to decide if we were going to take it with us. At this point, and for the first time, we opened the box. Lying on the top was a magazine, face down. In the top right-hand corner was a graphic of a red rosette on which was written, ***'WANTED: Teacher and Engineer – Burkina Faso'****.*

That got our attention! We picked up the magazine and turned it over – it was an old edition of 'Worldwide' published by a group called WEC International. We thought and prayed about it. We saw that this might be an opportunity, so we decided to ring WEC head office. At this point, we had never heard of WEC, and the magazine was a few years old, so when we rang, the conversation went something like this:

'Is this WEC?'

'Yes. How can I help you?'

'Do you still exist?'

'Yes, we are still quite active …'

Little were we aware of the scale of the activities of WEC International, a global mission movement focused on 'reaching unreached people.'

We learnt quickly, and within six weeks we were on a flight to spend two years at WEC's school for missionaries' children in Senegal, West Africa. The Burkina Faso role had been filled, but there were similar vacancies in Senegal.

This personal example shows that God can get the attention of even the most naïve and immature people. In the six weeks between the dream and the plane, God continued to speak through many and various means to confirm and affirm His leading, both directly to us as a couple and through others. In the space of a very short period, we came to the profound conviction that God knows how to speak, that He can communicate with us as a couple, and He can do so in a way that we can understand.

All this happened in 1991.

Since then, we have sought God for His guidance in all the major questions of life – career, major purchases, and ministry roles. During that time, God has led us into numerous different things, and through a variety of different means – Bible college; youth ministry; schools ministry; re-training; teaching in the UK; back to Senegal; leadership roles in local churches and in WEC. We have relocated over 20 times in the UK, France and Senegal.

The sense of leading and guiding has been the same, whether God has led us into 'spiritual' ministry or 'secular' work. (We don't like this distinction because we believe that everything we do is spiritual – but we use it to support our point that we believe that the leading and guiding of God should be a function of all Christians' relationship with Him, and not restricted to those who want to engage in church or mission ministry.)

We all start the journey somewhere.

If you look back on your journey so far, how have you heard God speak?

How has He guided you?

If you want to go deeper, then it will be in small steps of listening and doing.

10 HAVING THE RIGHT MIND

'But we have the mind of Christ.'

1 Corinthians 2:16

Did you know that, as a Christian, you have the mind of Christ?

This is one of the most astounding statements in the Bible. In his first letter to the church in Corinth, the Apostle Paul makes an almost inconceivable statement. He writes, '*But we have the mind of Christ.*' 1 Corinthians 2:16.

Wait! What? I have the mind of Christ? We have the mind of Christ? Really?

First, let's take a step back and consider what Paul is NOT saying. He is not saying, 'I know everything, as God knows everything.' To have the mind of Christ does not mean that we suddenly have a mind akin to some cosmic Wikipedia, where we suddenly possess every answer to every question (even if some people think they do!).

What, then, does this statement mean, and why should it be such an encouragement to us?

Firstly, consider the context. In this passage Paul explains how the Holy Spirit searches the deep things of God and then reveals them to spiritual minds of spiritual people. Only people born again of the Spirit of God can discern these spiritual things. So, if you are born again, you have the capacity to discern the mind of God.

Secondly, Paul says, '***We** have the mind of Christ.*' He is talking to a group, not to a specific individual. Discernment is an individual activity carried out within a group in which all have the capacity, the privilege and the responsibility to discern together what the Spirit is saying. Discernment is not the preserve of one or two special people within the Body of Christ; it is a gift for all.

At the same time, we must ensure that our pride does not allow us to think that we, of all Christians, have been given a unique revelation that no-one else can discern.

Spiritual people can discern spiritual things – and they can do it together. If all of our motivations, actions and expectations are in order, then we can confidently submit what we believe the Spirit is saying into whatever expression of the Body of Christ that we are part of, to give the group the chance to affirm and confirm what they believe the Spirit is saying. We don't need to convince anyone of anything; the Spirit is well able to do that.

Thirdly, Paul says, '*We* ***have*** *the mind of Christ.*' Present tense. As long as we have the Spirit in us, then we possess this capacity to know the mind of God. The Spirit's presence in our lives guarantees our adoption as sons and daughters (2 Corinthians 12:2).

As there can be no dispute about the fact that we have the Spirit in us, so it settles the questions that we have the mind of Christ. Paul does not say, 'We had it' (as if it only related to our salvation), nor does he say, 'We will have it' (as if it is something we will gain in the future once we have matured a little bit, or read through the whole of the Bible, or passed some theological education).

Therefore, discernment and knowing the will of God are within the capacity of every Christians. Where the Spirit is, there the capacity to discern the mind of God is.

Finally, Paul says, '*We have* ***the mind of Christ.***' As mentioned before, this does not mean that the entire counsel of God's wisdom has been downloaded into our finite minds – we obviously could not contain it! But it does mean that we have the faculties, by His Spirit, to perceive, to understand, to judge and to determine the wisdom of God.

As Christians, we have the capacity. Spiritual people can discern spiritual things – whether mature or immature in faith, adult, young person or child, from any culture, from any generation, from any professional, educational or theological training.

With that encouragement ringing in our hearts and minds, let's move on.

11 HAVING THE RIGHT HEART

'Do not conform to the patterns of this world but be transformed by the renewing of your mind. Then you will be able to test and approve what God's will is – his good, pleasing and perfect will.'

Romans 12:2

Are you attentive to the voice of God?

To develop intimacy, sensitivity and discernment we need to have the right heart. In the Bible the heart can refer to the organ that pumps blood around the body. But the heart can also refer to the entirety of our being — our emotions, our reason, and our will. It is the hidden spring which motivates all our actions, whether they are good or evil. The attitude of the heart plays a crucial role in hearing from God, and it can be a fruitless source of frustration to earnestly seek God if our hearts are not in the right place to receive what He has to say.

Beware - we enter now into the territory of heart surgery!

In all seriousness, you might read through the next chapter and feel condemned, worthless or that you have completely missed the mark. So, before you embark, we want to arm you.

Firstly, don't stop reading in this chapter. In the next chapter we will explain how to use your reflections as a springboard to jump into a completely renewed relationship with God.

Secondly, we are talking here about the quality and intimacy of your walk with God, NOT whether you are saved. If you are a Christian and feel challenged by what you read, then celebrate the fact that the Spirit is alive in you! He yearns for you to go deeper, spend more time with Him, be more intimate and discover the plans and purposes He has for you. This is a good thing.

It is the Father's heart that draws you, so be sensitive and let Him draw you.

To begin with, let's consider some reasons why our hearts might NOT be in the right place.

We believe we already know what to do. This is when we come to God to ask Him to bless what we have already decided to do. This is marginally better that pushing ahead regardless, but it is not the same as letting Him lead you in your decision-making from the very outset.

In James chapter 4:13-17, we are warned about an approach to planning our lives that takes no heed of God. The Bible calls our human plans 'boasting' and 'evil'. That is quite a stark warning. As Christians, we are to look to Him for His leading and guidance. It is the only right way to live. All things should be brought to Him in prayer to determine if our choice is His will for us. Once all is settled in this way, everything that we decide to do will come from a place of Spirit-led conviction.

The reasons for following this pattern are self-evident. God knows everything; we do not. He knows the end from the beginning; we do not. He has plans and purposes to bless us and extend the Kingdom; we don't know them. Again, what we see sketched in the pages of scripture is an invitation to a life in Christ that reflects a continual, intimate relationship – God leads and guides, we listen and obey. This should be the norm for all Christians.

The Bible has a word for when we think we know better than God – it's called pride. It's a sin! But there is hope – keep reading!

Our lives are not rightly ordered. There are things that occupy our life, our time, our thinking and our affections. We attach ourselves to them, give them importance and we organise our lives around them. They become our priorities. Everyone lives life in this way. These things may be good or bad. They might include our marriage, our children, and our career. Or they might include our hobbies, art, music, or running. Or they might include our spare time activities, social media, reading, watching TV, etc.

There are two ways to try and discover what your affections are. Firstly, take stock of your life and ask yourself:

What do I spend most of my time thinking about or doing?

What do I give importance to in my life?

What takes priority?

Compile a list of these things. Your top ten!

The second step is slightly more difficult but try and be as honest as you can. Where in this list would you place your relationship with God? Be honest. If it helps, ask yourself the three questions again and see where God comes in terms of time and priority.

Now consider, 'Where should God be on the list?'

Of course, the Creator of all things should be Number One! That is where He alone deserves to be. But all too often we find He is replaced by other things that grab our attention.

As mentioned earlier, many of the things on our lists will not be 'evil', and that is one reason why it is so difficult to keep Him at Number One. For example, if you are married, it might not seem unusual to have your spouse at the top. Or, if you have been blessed with loving parents or beautiful children and grandchildren these too may come at the top. However wonderful they are, in an ordered life, they should not be Number One. God should. You might find that offensive, but, when our life is ordered properly and God is Number One, then we are in a much better place to love the people who are in our lives. Therefore, with God at Number One we are able to love and care for our spouses, parents, children or grandchildren much more ably than if we tried to put them at Number One.

Now, this relates to the good things in your life, but what about the things on your list that you really have no need for, or that may even be bad for you?

If you have no time for God because you are up all night partying or if you spend so much time on social media that you never pray, then some changes are needed. If you are serious about growth in the area of discernment and your walk with God, then sometimes you will have to make changes. Remove or re-adjust things – do whatever it takes to make sure that God is Number One and that He remains there.

Reflect on this list often. Our affections are not static. The list you write today may not be the same or in the same order as the list you might write in six months' time. Therefore, it is a constant work to monitor your life and order it aright. Keep God at the top, keep your focus on Him, and keep looking to Him. Don't let yourself get side-tracked, distracted, or blinkered, because this robs you of the privilege of walking closely with God.

The Bible has a word for when God is NOT Number One – it's called idolatry. It's a sin! But there is hope – keep reading!

We are not willing. The Cambridge English Dictionary defines willingness as 'being happy to do something if it is needed'. Conversely, to be unwilling is 'to not want to do something'. When God speaks, we might find that we are unwilling to do what He is asking. The question of whether we are willing is always answered within a context. There are consequences to every choice. If there were no consequences, then we presume that most Christians would be willing to follow whatever God said to them. But there are consequences to every decision that we make. Reflection on these consequences is sometimes called 'counting the cost'. This is a healthy thing to do. It becomes unhealthy when it moves us away from obedience to God.

We once spent a long time coaching a couple through a process of discernment. It began because they had the deep gnawing sense that there was something different that they should be doing. They were experiencing what it was like to be stirred up by God. So, they began to seek God and as they did so it became clear that God was leading them into something new.

There were some huge signposts along the way that confirmed that they should leave their job and relocate to another area of the UK to engage in a different type of ministry. It was clear to them, to their church and to us what God was saying.

Initially, they were enthusiastic and embraced this, and began to take steps in the direction that they were being called. However, as the implications for these steps began to reveal themselves, rather than embrace them and work through them, they began to question the call.

Whilst they were counting the cost, they were presented with an alternative option that would require much less upheaval. They decided to take that route. No-one else shared their conviction that this was the right thing to do and counselled them accordingly, but they determined to do it anyway. We then watched as they drifted for a long time. Years in fact. They never really found contentment in anything. Our experience is that this is quite common.

We believe that our willingness should be determined by

the worth of the One who is asking, and NOT by the cost of the decision to follow. God is of ultimate worth, everything else should pale into insignificance. In fact, it is often in the crunch decisions that we truly see where our affections lie.

Pauline writes:

When we were asked by WEC to return to the school in Senegal for a second time, my natural instinct was to say, 'No way!' Not only was it my natural instinct but, by now, we had three children, we had a lovely house, good jobs, and a good church.

When we first received the request (in a letter), I was very surprised to note that my response was not immediate dismissal, but rather, 'I'll pray about it'. This in itself was a miracle and a sign that perhaps this was God speaking.

Over the following weeks, John and I prayed and talked about it – with each other; with the children; and with people whose wisdom we trusted. We also gathered lots of information about what life would be like for us as a family living at the school.

As the weeks went by, I noticed a peace. This had to be from God. I also noticed how positive John and the children were. Eventually, with a big gulp, we decided that it was right to go back.

When I arrived back in Senegal, I struggled. Big time. I found myself in a very dark place, and this led me to doubt God's very existence. Hadn't God led us here? If so, why was it so hard? I felt that I'd been tricked by God into being back there. But the God that I thought I believed in would not trick people, so maybe there wasn't a God after all. How ironic! There I was, a missionary in Africa, questioning whether God was real!

With hindsight, I can now see that God allowed this crisis in order to show me what was really in my heart. Had you asked me back in the UK if I trusted God, I would have said, 'Of course!' But having arrived in Senegal and suffering from severe culture shock, I realized that I didn't trust God at all. I thought He had either made a big mistake or wasn't real at all!

At this point I had a choice. I could either give up and walk away from God altogether, or I could persevere, ask my questions and find the answers.

The school happened to have the 'Alpha Course' in a set of videos, so I began to watch them. I went right back to basics. Was there a God? Was Jesus real?

I came out the other side of that time of searching with a much stronger faith, a greater understanding of who God is and who I am in Christ. The struggle led to growth.

Did that make all the trauma of culture shock go away? No. The trauma lasted for years. But I was able to persevere in His strength knowing that we were there in obedience to Him and trusting that He knew the best place for our family.'

The point of sharing this story is to say that we understand the cost of being willing.

Just because God makes clear what He wants us to do does not necessarily mean that it's all going to work out in the way we expect it to or would like.

Pain free. Cost free.

We know that sometimes the cost of following His leading is very high. It might even mean giving up our very lives.

For this reason, being convinced of God's leading in the discernment process is critical if we are going to be able to persevere in faith when the going gets tough. We also want to say that whilst counting the cost is an important part of the process, it should not be the primary factor of our decision-making.

If we go through the process of counting the cost and decide that we are not willing to follow God's leading, then the Bible has a name for this. It is disobedience, whether active (doing what we know we should not do) or passive (not doing what we know we should do). Disobedience is a sin. But there is hope – keep reading!

We are fearful of the consequences. In the UK everyone blames Health and Safety for ruining much of our fun. To be fair, it can go too far. But, when you're stood on top of six 50-gallon oil barrels, stacked on top of one another, simultaneously swaying and wobbling whilst trying to weld two steel beams together (as John has) you gain a greater appreciation of the benefits that safety has to health!

John isn't a great fan of heights. If he stands at the top of a cliff, he develops an irrational and overwhelming desire to jump off. In this sense, fear is rational. It keeps us from putting ourselves in harm's way, or it at least raises our adrenalin levels so that if we find we are in harm's way we are better prepared to react!

When we went back to Senegal the second time, we went with our three children aged between two and six. To some people this was irresponsible. How could we take them to such a dangerous environment? Away from health care. Away from all the things that they would have if they remained in the UK. Away from family? How could we ruin their lives, their education and their prospects?

We too wondered what effect taking our children to Senegal would have on their lives and well-being. But we chose to trust that God cared about them more than we ever could.

In our spiritual lives, fear can hinder our capacity to receive and obey God. We have a choice in our walk with God - to either walk by fear or to walk by faith. If our lives are constantly shaped by fear, then the sphere of our lives shrinks into a smaller and smaller existence. On the other hand, faith releases us into expansive lives in Christ. That is the reward of a life of faith.

Pauline recounts a testimony that stemmed from her fear of being away from home.

As a child, any amount of time away from home was stressful for me. Even going to my best friend's house for a one-night sleepover would make me feel physically sick. Going on holiday with friends; going away to university – all very stressful. Imagine how I felt then, when we were first presented with the need for an engineer and a teacher in Senegal! Surely God wasn't asking this of me! There were literally thousands and thousands of people who would be better suited to this than me! God would have to make this blindingly clear if there was to be any chance of me getting on a plane to Africa.

But God knows me better than I know myself, and so He knew exactly how to speak to me. Through numerous ways things became clear, to the point that I had peace and knew that this was what God was asking us to do. I didn't like it, and I didn't want it, but it was undeniably God, so I had to pay attention. I knew that if I was calling Him 'Lord', then I couldn't at the same time pick and choose what bits of His calling I chose to obey.

Throughout the Bible there are two wonderful phrases that occur many times. '*Fear not…*' and '*Don't be afraid…*' And often they are accompanied with a promise '… *for I am with you.*' The key to dispel fear is to trust – trust in the One who is with you.

To be fearful is to place the object of our fear as bigger, stronger, greater than God. This is sin, but there is hope – keep reading!

We want what the world wants. In a prayer to His Father in Heaven, Jesus said of His disciples, '*I have given them your word and the world has hated them, for they are not of the world any more than I am of the world*' (John 17:14). As disciples, just like the first disciples, we are called to be 'in the world' but not 'of the world.'

What does that mean?

If we are not of the world, then what are we? As followers of Jesus, Christians are 'of the Kingdom of God'. We live in the 'now and the not yet' of the Kingdom. In other words, in the here and now, we are called to live out our lives with different values, aims and purposes. And at the same time, we know that there is so much more awaiting us in eternity.

Jesus spent much of His time teaching people what this meant. In His Sermon on the Mount Jesus outlines radical values for living. He explains how much of the promised blessing of God is released through a lifestyle that is suited for the Kingdom. His explicit direction is, '*Do not worry, saying, "What shall we eat?" or "What shall we drink?" or "What shall we wear?" … But seek first His kingdom and his righteousness and all these things will be given to you as well*' (Matthew 6:31&33).

This is a blunt, direct, and clear instruction. Have we lost sight of this simplicity in the modern age? Are these words of Jesus somehow no longer relevant? Have we replaced God's wisdom with human wisdom?

Ask yourself this. What counsel did you receive as you grew up? Or what counsel have you passed on to your children? Was it that the most important thing to do is to seek first the Kingdom, whatever that might mean for you? Or was it that the most important thing is to get a good education, get a good career, buy a house, make provision for yourself for when you are older, do the things that you enjoy doing and in the time that you have left over, do something for God?

It is not that these things are wrong, or that Christians should not do these things; rather it is wrong when they become our primary motivation. We have heard many well-meaning Christians who think that they are earnestly seeking God for His purposes, when really all they are doing is seeking His blessing upon their own purposes. This is fundamentally different, and really expresses a lust for the world, rather than a desire to seek first the Kingdom.

We have heard many people make well-meaning wonderful promises about how, once they are wealthy enough, they will use the money to invest in the Kingdom. That is a noble intention – but few are the people who continue to live simple lives and invest their wealth sacrificially, into the Kingdom of God. What we do with the little we have is indicative of what we will do with a lot.

Let's be liberated – let's come to God with genuinely open hands and seek first the Kingdom. Lord, what do you want me to do with my life, my time, my possessions?

Let's liberate our children and new Christians.

Let's think very carefully about what we multiply in our discipleship.

Let's release a generation of radical, faith-filled, Kingdom-minded Christians who will risk all to serve God, rather than try to create comfort zones, mitigate risk, and make faith safe.

The former releases the power and blessing of God; the latter is boring and insipid and demonstrably turns the next generation away from faith.

Of course, it does! Who wants a faith that is merely a thin Christian veneer laid over a life that is otherwise completely the same as the world?

Let's live this.

Let's model this to those around, especially our children and future generations of Christians.

Let's multiply this!

The Bible has a word for desiring the world rather than the Kingdom – it's called lust. It's a sin. But there is hope – keep reading!

12 LIVING WITH CONVICTION

'I will give you a new heart and put a new spirit in you.'

Ezekiel 36:26

Are you ready to start afresh?

Thanks for not giving up and reading through to this point.

We deliberately wanted to emphasise some of the factors that might hinder us from discerning God and name it as SIN. We know that it is not a popular word, and no-one likes to be called a sinner. But if we call it sin, rather than leaving it un-named, it is much easier to deal with.

Look at all this sin potentially affecting the condition of our hearts – what are we going to do about it? Where can we go from here? Is there any hope for us? Yes, much! And it lies in the wonderful gift called repentance.

We like the way that the author of Genesis personifies sin when he wrote about God speaking to Cain. Cain was having a battle. He was faced with jealousy, was struggling with anger, and was feeling downcast. In response to this, God challenged him as to why he felt like that. God said, *'If you do what is right, will you not be accepted? But if you do not do what is right sin is crouching at your door; it desires to have you, but you must rule over it'* (Genesis 4:6).

We too have decisions and choices to make. But we can approach this on a completely different footing to Cain. For we have Christ in us. And because of that, we can be empowered by Him to choose NOT to sin, and to decide NOT to continue in sin. *'For we know that our old self was crucified with him so that the body ruled by sin might be done away with, that we should no longer be slaves to sin – because anyone who has died has been set free from sin'* (Romans 6:6-7).

These truths should liberate us. In calling out the disordered parts of our lives for what they are, sin, we have a perfect solution. The work of Christ makes perfect provision to deal with the consequences of sin, and we can know forgiveness and restoration, and start again with a clean sheet. And, whilst sin may still crouch at our door, because of Christ, this sin need no longer have power over us.

Don't be frightened to let the Holy Spirit do the deep work of highlighting any issues of pride, idolatry, disobedience, fear and lust. Recognise them, call them out, confess them, repent, and then seek to live differently. All of this is the fruit and blessing that comes from earnestly seeking to know and do the will of God.

Let's look at an example from scripture of how this journey works.

The teaching of Jesus to all Christians is very plain and easy to understand. He said, '*Whoever wants to be my disciple must deny themselves and take up their cross and follow me*' (Luke 9:23).

The Apostle Paul was one of the early Christians who understood this. He took this truth to heart and declared it to others. It was his justification for what he did, and how he lived his life - '*I have been crucified with Christ and I no longer live, but Christ lives in me. The life I now live in the body, I live by faith in the Son of God, who loved me and gave Himself for me'* (Galatians 2:20).

There is a lot that could be written about what it means to be a disciple, but in relation to the scope of this book, the teaching we have explored about how we seek, listen, and obey the voice of God is one key area. Living like this is an expression of life, of worship, of devotion, of commitment. It is a demonstration that the ownership of a life has changed. It is no longer I, but Christ!

There is a world of difference between coming to God with full hands, busy lives, fixed plans and asking, 'Lord, please bless what I am doing', and coming to God with empty hands and asking, 'Lord, what do you want me to do?' One approach is essentially closed; the other invites God to speak freely, expansively, with no pre-conceived idea of what the answer is going to be.

But how do we get into that place? We make sure our hearts are in the right place. Unless we do, the process of seeking God can be a very frustrating experience. It can cause us to miss out on the very thing we want, and the very words that God wants to say.

This open attitude enabled Paul to declare with confidence that he was, '*Paul, a servant of Christ Jesus, called to be an Apostle and set apart for the Gospel of God*' (Romans 1:1).

How would you introduce yourself?

If we were asked that today, we would be at peace to say, *'John/Pauline, a servant of Christ, called to be a leader and set apart for the unreached peoples of the world.'*

As you read this today, could you complete the following sentence by filling in the blanks: *'[NAME] a servant of Christ Jesus, called to be [......] and set apart for [......]'?*

If not, then read on – we earnestly believe that it is God's promise and your privilege to be able to complete that sentence with sincere conviction.

If we all genuinely asked God for His counsel and for His guidance, we believe that two things would happen.

Firstly, He would either affirm the rightness of what you are currently doing, or He would tell you what He wants you to do. Either way, you will be armed with the confirmation and assurance that this is what God wants you to do.

Secondly, the whole church would be full of people whose normal practice was to walk with Him in an intimate way and to listen to Him speak. We would, therefore, be a responsive people. Into these hearts, minds and lives God would then guide us and direct us. We would be a people who would have the confidence to stand in Christ, in whatever context we find ourselves, because of the foundation of knowing that we are where God wants us. This certainty would release faith to pray for the fulfilment of God's promises to provide all we need for what He has asked us to do.

How much more fruitful would we be!

This is the garden life that we believe we are all called to. God saying to us - *Walk with me – I've got something for you to do over here or show me what you've been doing in this piece of the garden I've given you to tend.*

The best place for anyone to be is in the centre of God's plans and purposes for them. He rules and He reigns over all things, and that includes us.

How often have you prayed God's prayer?

'Our Father in heaven, hallowed be your name, your kingdom come, your will be done, on earth as it is in heaven' (Matthew 6:9-10).

As you have prayed this, we are sure you have done so in hope that God answers, but how did you expect God to answer this prayer? Is the Kingdom and His will all related to someone else, rather than related to you personally? Is your hope that your own country will become more like the Kingdom, that the Church will become more effective, and that more people will be impacted with the Gospel? In other words, are all the applications of this prayer external to you?

But hang on a minute - are you not part of this earth? Do you stand apart from the earth that you are asking God to conform to His will? No.

As we genuinely seek God for the coming of His Kingdom on earth as it is in heaven, it must have a personal application.

Lord, please save us from the 'change them but leave me alone' type of prayer! Instead, our prayers should be, *'All is Yours, Lord, including me. The earth is the LORD's and everything in it … it's yours, I'm yours … Lord, Your will be done, in my life on earth as it is in heaven.'*

He lovingly rules over us all, over our days, over our time, over our life, and all that we have or ever will possess. So, let's participate with him in the coming of His Kingdom. Let it come in us, as well as through us.

The Lordship of Christ over us should not be an obscure, abstract truth that bears little relationship to anything that we do or say, or any decisions that we make regarding our lives, our time, and our possessions. Rather, it should be a great liberation that we receive and enjoy.

Lord, please give us grace to understand these things and to have healthy hearts so that we can be sensitive to Your voice!

13 HOW MIGHT GOD SPEAK?

'But when he, the Spirit of truth, comes, he will guide you into all truth. He will not speak on his own; he will speak only what he hears, and he will tell you what is to come.'

John 16:13

What should we expect to hear from God?

This is a really important question. What we expect we are more likely to perceive. We all grow up with different expectations, and we may each come to this question with some very strong convictions. If our minds are too fixed, and if we believe that God can ONLY speak in a particular way, we risk missing what He has to say.

Here are some of our thoughts, offered in the hope that they will help you to see that God can speak. And that He will speak as, when, and however He wants to. The experiences and stories that we have included are given as examples of how it might happen. They are not to be taken as normative – God is just far too creative for that.

We have divided the following list into what we will label Primary, Secondary and Tertiary means. This is because whilst God may choose to use any of these means of communication, we should not give them equal weight. Indeed, we should use the Primary means to weigh, consider and check everything that we believe God is saying through either the Secondary or Tertiary means.

Primary Means

An audible voice. Should God choose to speak to you directly, in such a way that His voice is audible, we believe you will be in no doubt that it is Him! And with this certainty, you will probably find it relatively easy to obey! That said, this is an extremely rare occurrence. Personally, we do not know anyone who has had this experience, but we have read testimony of those who have, and we can also read of this happening in the pages of scripture. However, be careful not to misinterpret what is written in the Bible. We can read the words, 'God said…' many times, and we can read about how God spoke to different people at different times, but unless it explicitly describes an audible voice, there is no reason to attribute God's speaking as an audible voice. In the book of Numbers 12:6-8 it clearly states that Moses alone, of all the prophets, was a man to whom God spoke *'face-to-face, clearly and not in riddles'*.

This certainly does not preclude God from speaking audibly, and it might even be your experience, but we do want to stress that it is very rare, and an inestimable privilege for any who have had that experience.

The Bible. The Bible is the richest source of guidance and contains a wealth of treasure. The more familiar we become with it, the more we will be able to discern God's mind. Thankfully, we do not need to be scholars in Hebrew and Greek to be able to access it! As English speakers it is such a privilege to have the Bible in our own heart language (a privilege that many around the world still do not have).

So, how does He use the Bible to speak to us?

There are some complex issues around the theme of the inspiration of Scripture. Our starting point is that we take the Bible to be inspired by the Holy Spirit, written by people in a specific context, entirely trustworthy and that it is the final authority in matters of faith and behaviour. We also believe that the Holy Spirit has come to guide us into all truth (John 16:13).

So, the Word and the Spirit work together to guide and shape our lives. And this is a powerful dynamic.

On the one hand, you may experience the Holy Spirit bringing a scripture to mind, or a particular verse somehow 'jumping off the page' as you read a passage. We don't discount these experiences in any way. Indeed, we have been blessed in these ways ourselves. On the other hand, it is important to remember that all the Bible is the Word of God. So, we should not ignore passages that have not been 'quickened/illumined' (or whatever word your church tradition might use) to you.

We don't need to 'feel' that a verse of scripture is important for it to be important. For example, when the Apostle John quotes Jesus' teaching, '*Remain in me, as I also remain in you. No branch can bear fruit by itself; it must remain in the vine. Neither can you bear fruit unless you remain in me*' (John 15:4), this piece of teaching is important to you. All the time!

However, it might be that on one occasion, as you read through the Gospel of John, the Holy Spirit emphasises this verse to you, or brings it to mind as you pray for yourself or someone else. If that happens, you would do well to pay attention and respond. But, even if you do not have that experience, you should apply this teaching to your life and 'remain' in God if you want to have a fruitful life.

At the same time, God can give revelation about things that do not specifically appear in scripture. For example, how did we know that God was leading us to Senegal? Or how did we know that He was asking us to sell our house and trust Him for what we needed? There is no specific mention of Senegal or our house in the Bible, but He still used it to guide us in both these decisions.

How did He do that?

In 1998, we were asked to consider the possibility of a return to Senegal to serve with WEC at a school that serves families engaged in mission work across the whole of West Africa.

Lord, should we go?

We began the process of discernment by committing ourselves to His will and asked Him for guidance. We tried to listen to make the right decision. We sought to have the right attitude in our hearts and created the space for Him to lead and guide us.

Then, one night, as John was reading through Galatians as part of his normal reading, he read the following verse: '*Therefore, as we have opportunity, let us do good to all people, especially to those who belong to the family of believers*' (Galatians 6:10).

Again, this teaching applies to all Christians, but at this moment, at his desk in our home, the Holy Spirit used it as a trigger to release him to say, 'Yes Lord! You are calling us.' This was part of the process of leading us as a family.

Given that the audible voice is a very rare experience, it follows that the Bible should play a core, and crucial, role in every Christian's life as they take steps to discern God's leading. We don't say that to limit or discount the freedom for God to bring guidance through other means, but rather that when guidance comes through another means, it should always be tested against Scripture. God will never lead us in a way that is contrary to His Word, and so to be familiar with the Word is crucial. This helps us to discern what God is saying to us and to help others in discerning what God is saying to them.

Secondary Means

These are other ways by which the Holy Spirit may speak to us. Scripture says that one of Holy Spirit's primary roles is to '*guide [us] into all truth. He will not speak on his own; he will speak only what he hears [from the Father], and he will tell you what is to come'* (John 16:13). Therefore, we should expect the Holy Spirit to lead and guide, and we should become increasingly familiar with His voice as we grow in our relationship with God.

How does the Holy Spirit speak? We find the answer in Scripture.

By calling them secondary means we are not in any way demoting the Holy Spirit below the Bible. However, the Bible is the gift of God to help us test what we believe the Holy Spirit might be saying to us. The Holy Spirit inspired the Bible – He would not say something directly to us that would contradict scripture. That would be inconsistent. So, by secondary we mean that the Bible is entirely trustworthy and always validates and affirms the other diverse means by which the Holy Spirit might lead and guide.

Dreams and Visions. Jacob had a dream (Genesis 28); Joseph had dreams (Genesis 37 & 40); prophets had dreams (Numbers 12); King Solomon had a dream (1 Kings 3:15). The prophecy in Revelation tells us that in the last days in which we live and await Jesus' return, the outpouring of the Holy Spirit will cause '*old men to dream dreams*' (prophesied in Joel 2:28 and fulfilled in Acts 2:17). We've heard many testimonies of Muslims having dreams about Jesus. As recounted earlier, we have been guided by dreams.

Through a dream, God may present something to you in a manner that attracts your attention, or He might reveal something that you have been unconsciously thinking about. Beware though. We all dream, but not every dream will have significance. Sometimes we dream because our mind is preoccupied with something, or because we've eaten some cheese too close to bedtime!

Not all dreams are Holy Spirit-inspired, but some may be. Often, the dreams inspired by the Holy Spirit are more vivid, clear and more memorable than 'normal' dreams. They tend not to evaporate into the mist of your waking moments like other dreams. Again, not all vivid, clear, memorable dreams are Spirit-inspired, but some may be. In any case, if you have the experience of a vivid dream, record the detail of it as soon as possible so that you have a record for future reflection.

A vision might be described as an impression that comes to you in the same way that a dream would – except when you are awake.

These dreams and visions may speak of what will be. In this sense they contain potential. They are best seen as guidance, and as invitations to participate in God's work. In other words, what you see in this kind of dream or vision may not become your lived experience unless you respond to the invitation. God will still accomplish what He plans to do, with or without you. This truth should lead us not to indifference, but rather to a passionate desire to be a part of what God invites us into through a dream or a vision. Or they may be God's way of grabbing our attention (as in our case with the dream John had inviting him to work in Bath, Belfast or Burkina Faso). They may be God's way of helping us be more attentive to the Spirit's guiding.

Spiritual gifts. In 1 Corinthians 12 we read about the gifts of the Spirit. These are the manifestation of the Holy Spirit through the members of the local church and are given to us by God for the good of the whole Body.

In this passage, Paul writes within the context of a worship service, but the manifestation of the gifts of the Spirit is not limited to collective times of worship. For example, we may experience a message of wisdom, a message in tongues, an interpretation, or a prophecy outside of that context. And, whilst the gift is given for the common good, this does not preclude the gift being given for our own personal guidance.

The gifts of the Spirit are not manifest solely for the blessing of the members of a church. We have had numerous experiences, when praying for people who are not Christians, where the Spirit has imparted a word of wisdom to us that, as we shared it with others, has turned out to be a wonderful key that unlocks someone's heart to the reality of God.

Inner witness. This is quite a difficult thing to explain. How do you explain conviction? Burden? Presence? It is hard to describe, but you just know when you know. The burden that God carries for all His creation would obviously be too much for us to bear. However, God does share some of His burden with us in small measures to lead and guide our thoughts and decisions. For us, why do our hearts ache for unreached peoples, and especially those in West Africa, but not as much for widows and orphans specifically? For others, serving widows and orphans is a deep life-long passion. Some people just love children's work; others try and avoid it like the plague!

Personal passion is not an issue of access or experience. It is to do with how we were made, and with how God has shared some of His heart. We do not long for the unreached to hear about Jesus as much as God does, and others do not long for widows and orphans to be cared for as much as God. But, by sharing some of His heart with us, He motivates us to move our lives in a particular direction.

It is a huge privilege to have the Spirit of God live inside us, and through that indwelling, we are moved by love. It is relational; it is inexplicable; it is undeniably a work of God, and we should be alert to His leading and guiding in this way.

What breaks your heart? What burdens you? For what do you have particular compassion? What makes you angry?

The Apostle Paul wrote that it was Christ's love that compelled him (2 Corinthians 5:14). So, what would this look like for you? Let the Spirit have His way and let the love of Christ compel you.

In sound engineering there is a principle called resonance. A particular frequency of sound can cause an object to vibrate (resonate) if it is the same as that object's natural frequency. You might experience this in a car if the engine idles at a frequency that makes your stomach feel unwell! This is the principle at work when you tune guitar strings relative to one another. It is a good metaphor for what we can experience when God shares some of His heart with us – it causes our heart to resonate and, as it were, beat in tune with His. We feel as He feels; we are burdened as He is burdened.

Other Christians. As mentioned earlier, God has called us into a body, the family of God. Our faith is intended to be a communal faith and, as a community of believers, it can only be lived out in the context of the body.

We are not called to live independent lives, but interdependent ones. That is God's design.

This is practically outworked during the discernment process. There is only one Spirit, and He indwells each of us. It stands to reason, therefore, that He is able to communicate with us both directly and indirectly. In fact, in the matter of discernment it is crucial that we take account of what the appropriate people around us are saying. Those we trust; those who share our primary commitment to seek first the Kingdom and who hold this as a priority; those who have a proven record of wisdom and of discernment. These will be invaluable allies in our pursuit of discerning God's leading, and we can be invaluable allies for those doing the same.

What are others saying to us?

What do they see in us?

Do they affirm what we think God is saying to us?

Do we affirm what they think God is saying to them?

It requires a level of humility and vulnerability to be open to what the Spirit is saying through others, and it requires a level of diligence to seek God earnestly and honestly on behalf of others.

Finally, it requires courage. As you discern God's voice, you may grapple with whether you want to do what you think God is calling you to. But, as you count the cost, it is always good to involve others in what you think God is saying.

Angels. This is not something that is commonly talked about in churches around the world. We must be wary and reject any unbiblical practice such as 'channelling angels' or of 'worshipping angels' in any guise. At the same time, we cannot ignore the reality of the presence of angels in Scripture, nor the way in which God uses them to speak to His people.

They are mentioned throughout the pages of both the Old and New Testaments. In the book of Acts and in the Epistles, angels are mentioned in the build-up to Jesus' life, during His life and after His death and resurrection. And prophecy in the Bible, especially the book of Revelation, tells us they will play a crucial role in the end times. It would also seem from scripture that some angels are clearly heavenly in appearance, whilst others can be confused for other people. (Compare Hebrews 13:2 with the experience of the shepherds at the birth of Christ in Luke 2:9.) They are described by the author of Hebrews as, '*ministering spirits sent to serve those who will inherit salvation*' Hebrews 1:14.

One way in which they serve is to share messages from God to His people. We have had no personal experience of hearing from an angel, and neither do we personally know anyone who has. However, we are aware that there are those throughout Church history and in contemporary times who have.

Tertiary Means

In this category we have basically included any other means that God may use. Again, this is not an exhaustive or normative list, and there are numerous other examples that you might be able to include. God knows how to get our attention and how to communicate. These are what we might call 'signposts'. They are ways in which God can make us sit up, take note, and in that moment bring some conviction of the Spirit's leading on any matter or decision.

Nature. John writes:

I took a walk on the wilds of Dartmoor at a point in my life where I was feeling a bit stuck. We had just returned from our first 2 years in Senegal. I knew that there were significant decisions coming about my future career. I did not know which way was the best way to go and had no real conviction one way or another. Should I go back to engineering, or retrain to be a teacher? As I walked up one of the numerous hills, all that I could see ahead was the outline of the hill. Beyond that, all I could see was sky. Eventually, as I reached the summit of the hill and was able to look over, I could see the land spreading out before me in all its raw and natural beauty. The Spirit seized the moment to show me that I should walk into a new landscape for my life. He did this simply by imparting a clear thought to me at an opportune time.

Following this experience, we talked and prayed together, and sensed that this was God's leading. We shared it with others and prayed some more. When we had peace to continue, John made his application to teach. This led to a teaching post in the UK, three years of very rewarding work in a secondary school and then a move into teaching in Senegal with WEC. John didn't have all that in mind when he was climbing the hill on Dartmoor, but as God invited us on the journey, He had it all planned, and we simply had to follow Him step by step.

Opportunities. Sometimes, in our walk of faith we are presented with opportunities. Perhaps someone in church asks us to serve on one of the Sunday teams, or perhaps we are presented with a promotion at work, or we read of a post overseas that we are qualified to fulfil.

How do we know if we should say yes or no?

Some say that common sense should prevail unless you have a specific conviction one way or another. We are not at all convinced that this is true. Rather, we believe that our motivation should come from a conviction that something is the right thing to do. And, that in faith, we can trust God for that conviction.

Too often, 'common sense' is used as an excuse to eliminate the need to do the work of discernment. So, even if common sense might say, 'Of course it is good to serve in church' or 'Yes, this promotion is a good opportunity', we should still seek the mind of God about what He wants. We must give the space and time for God to speak into our decision-making before we make any decisions.

Why?

Because we want to know what He thinks about the opportunity. It may well be that, after going through a process of waiting and seeking, we believe it is right to take the opportunity – in which case, great. You move ahead with conviction. But equally, we might conclude that we shouldn't take the opportunity, in which case, great. You refuse it from a place of conviction. Either way, you have a stability in your decision-making that is born out of God's leading.

Circumstances. Learn to view circumstances in a similar way to opportunities. Things happen in life, and sometimes it can seem like circumstances force you to make certain decisions. Perhaps the loss of a job, the relocation of your office, or an unexpected health issue arises that means a certain decision is inevitable. But before you accept the 'inevitable', take a step back and ask God what He wants to say about it.

Conviction can release the faith needed to be able to push through the 'inevitable' and find an unexpected outcome. If we are people for whom circumstance is the loudest voice in our decision-making, then we are living impoverished lives; lives that are more fatalistic than relational. As we mentioned at the beginning, we believe that God has something to say into all areas of our lives, and so we should ask Him what that is.

What kind of thing might God want to say into a situation with a seemingly inevitable outcome? If there is no decision to make, the discernment is more to do with hearing truths from God that will encourage and strengthen us during the challenge – especially if the 'inevitable' is not pleasant or desired. Even if the outcome is that we accept the seemingly inevitable outcome of the circumstances, we can embrace it with joy, confidence, and conviction.

Once, John was presented with an opportunity to take up another role with a different organisation. He writes:

It was a perfect alignment of circumstance and opportunity. I knew that I was coming to the end of the role I was in, and this opportunity seemed a perfect fit for me. It would have used my gifts, it would have aligned with the family circumstances at the time, and it would have alleviated the pressure of facing uncertainty. All in all, it was quite exciting, and in unrelated conversations three different people encouraged me to apply. I found myself getting quite excited about this new possibility. What should I do?

What would you have done?

Considering the circumstances and opportunity, we could

have concluded that he should apply. But we didn't. We prayed. As we prayed over a period of weeks, two things began to happen.

Firstly, John's sense of excitement about the role began to diminish; it gradually faded away and evaporated. And secondly, his sense of peace that it was the right thing to do slowly diminished. This still left the question of what we should do next unresolved. But as we had no peace to pursue this particular opportunity, we decided not to apply.

Within weeks of making that decision, and as we continued to pray about the next steps, another opportunity opened. Again, we considered it, but it did not seem that it would be possible for us to fulfil the role that was being offered given our circumstances. This was a conundrum. We had peace about the opportunity, but the circumstances seemed to prohibit it. With that peace came the conviction to pursue the opportunity, and, as we pursued it, each of the circumstances that seemed to mitigate against it were resolved one by one. God can make a way where there seems to be no way!

Anything. Finally, we include this catch-all group. It includes such things as advertisements, news reports, donkeys (Numbers 22:28), hands appearing and writing on the wall (Daniel 5), music lyrics, books, biographies, casual conversations with a stranger. God can use literally anything to grab your attention and say something to you.

In 1995, after our first spell in Africa followed by a year in Bible College, we were back in Paignton. We felt led by God to establish a project in our local area. Our hope was that we would be able to work with local churches and Christian teachers to take the Gospel into schools, through helping with RE lessons, taking assemblies and having lunchtime clubs, etc.

It had not been an easy year. We had not been funded

well, and we had a young family. To gain some relevant experience, John had undertaken to work with a similar project in a nearby city. This necessitated a lot of travel up and down the dual carriageway.

Eventually, with the help of others, we were able to host a crunch meeting. At this meeting, the representatives of the key stakeholders met to discuss the project. At the end of the discussion, they were all very positive, and it was agreed that the project should go ahead.

The next day, John travelled up the dual carriageway in a very positive frame of mind, and later that day met with one of the people who had attended the meeting. After some general small talk, this man said, 'They love the project and want to move ahead … but they don't want you to lead it.'

John was gutted. Speechless. Stunned. Literally, everything we had been working towards for the past twelve months disappeared in that one short sentence. He left the office and began the drive back home.

John writes:

As I drove home, with tears I began to give voice to my raw emotions in prayer to God. 'How dare You! You have deceived us! All this hard work has come to nothing, and if this is what it means to follow You, then I am NEVER going to bother again!' It all came out! Then I stopped, and in an act of defiance I decided to stop praying, and to remove myself from His presence by turning on the radio.

The song 'One' by U2 came onto the radio. As Bono sang the words, 'Did I disappoint you? Or leave a bad taste in your mouth? You act like you never had love, and you want me to go without!'

The Spirit seized the moment and spoke into my embittered soul and broke me. Who was I? What was I doing? The Spirit poured balm on my hurt and enabled me to open my heart to Him again.

Obviously, Bono is not God! But the Spirit was able to speak through the song. Even as I write these words, I recall the depth of the emotions that I experienced in my car on that day. It's part of my journey.

[Just as a postscript to this story. It took us a while to get over this, but eventually we were able to focus afresh on seeking Him for the next step. Looking back, the group of people were right in their choice. They chose someone far better than we would have been, and the project thrives to this day. It also liberated us to do something else that we were far more suited to. So, we are very glad for what those people said, the decision they made, and God's leading and guiding. We also appreciate their courage to share that conviction with us, even though they knew it would hurt and cause us pain. God's will is perfect, even if it is not always easy to listen to.]

So, be alert and open to the voice of the Spirit, however it might come. He is a constant presence. He sometimes speaks in a loud voice, and sometimes in a 'still, small voice' (1 Kings 19:12).

It is our experience that the more intimate your relationship with God is, the more softly and gently He speaks to lead and to guide. He won't need to shout to get your attention if He already has it.

14 WHAT CAN I DO?

'Teach me to do your will, for you are my God; may your good Spirit lead me on level ground.'

Psalm 143:10

If we have taken steps to get our hearts in the right place, what else can we do to become a more discerning person?

We are going to let you into a little secret. We love each other! From the very first moment that we met, as students in Bristol, we have just felt nothing but love for each other. Yes, of course, we have our disagreements, and we argue, but underpinning all of that is a love that we find very easy. That is a wonderful blessing.

Having said that, even after all these years we don't fully know each other or always understand one another. However, we know each other better today than when we first met. It has been an absolute delight getting to know one another, and the more we have got to know one another, the more we have understood each other's likes and dislikes; how to make one another smile; what brings joy and what brings sadness. This has been a process of conversation, observation, and learning, but it has never been a chore. Our love has grown the more we have come to know one another. We haven't got to know each other because we must, or because it is expedient, or just because we think it is the right thing to do. We have done it because it has been our joy and delight.

In practice, getting to know someone takes time - conversation, working together, playing together and, in the case of parents, bringing up children together. There is no short-cut, and the journey of discovery is as much of a reward as the outcome. So today if you ask either of us what the other thinks or feels about something, then we are in a better place to tell you than we were when we first met.

When we first met, we were both fully present. In other words, all that there was to know about each other was already there. Getting to know one another has been a journey of discovery; a journey whereby we tell one another what we want and like (directly and indirectly), and as we express our opinions, approval, and disapproval.

We have also found that as time has gone on, we increasingly think about things in the same way and function as one couple, not as two individuals. It's a strange but beautiful thing.

This illustration from our marriage highlights a key point in the journey of becoming a more discerning person. Fundamentally, it is ALL about intimacy and relationship.

If we want to be able to answer the questions, 'What does God want me to do?', 'Does God want me to say something?' or 'What does God think about this?', then we have to look at our journey of deepening intimacy with Him, rather than see this as a mechanical process, or a clinical formula i.e., if we do A, B and C, then God will do D. It is far more relational and organic than that.

So, in terms of what you should do, we simply commend you to think about what makes you feel closer to God, and then give as much time and priority to that as you can.

And why wouldn't you?

The Creator, Sustainer and Father of all things wants to have a deepening relationship with you, and He wants to talk with you. Why would we put that off, or be indifferent to the riches that this truth promises us?

The following list of actions is not prescriptive nor exhaustive, but hopefully it gives you some ideas. As you read, ask yourself which you feel most inclined towards, and start with giving more time to that. Then as you reap the blessings of that, try and broaden your approach – you may be very surprised to find some unexpected blessings along the way.

Prayer. Prayer is dialogue. It's talking and it's listening. It's two-way. We wouldn't have got very far in our marriage if it had only ever been one of us talking to the other.

Prayer is a conversation, a dialogue, and sometimes it is also just being together and saying nothing. In our marriage just being together is a thing. And it is the same with God. We don't always have to be saying something when we are in His presence. Cultivate a relational approach to prayer — interceding, talking, listening throughout the day. Pray continually, 'Lord, what should we do here?', 'Lord, help me with this!', 'Lord, please bless this person I'm about to meet', 'Lord, what do you want me to say?', 'Lord, thank you for this.'

Worship. Worship is our response to recognizing the reality of who God is - His awesome glory, His love, His holiness, His justice, His truth. It is to reflect on those things and to humble ourselves before Him and communicate back to Him our wonder at who He is.

Whether you play an instrument, speak a prayer, sing, draw, or dance, it is a good thing to have regular times of praise, adoration, and worship - corporately as well as personally.

Whatever means and form you find most effectively releases you to rest in the presence of God, saturating yourself in Him – do that.

John writes:

Once, during a time of prayer and thanksgiving, I found myself kneeling before God – simply speaking out words of appreciation. From that place of worship, I felt as if I was being enveloped by the presence of God. It's hard to put such an experience into words, but I liken it to how I imagines it would feel to have warm treacle poured over me.

Worship, in whatever form, is a doorway which enables us to enter the presence of God. To connect more readily with the reality of His indwelling presence. This too should be a regular part of our walk with God.

Read the Bible. It IS the Word of God to you. It describes Him, it explains His purposes, it gives guidance for life. '*All scripture is God-breathed and is useful for teaching, rebuking, correcting and training in righteousness, so that the servant of God may be thoroughly equipped for every good work*' (2 Timothy 3:16-17).

Read it book by book; become familiar with it. If you prefer to listen to the Word, then do so with an audio Bible. If you find yourself wanting to know more, then get a commentary or a study Bible. But whatever you do, become immersed in the Word, and seek the guidance of the Holy Spirit to bring understanding and lead you into all truth.

Don't be content with reading a short verse and then spending the rest of your time reading the devotional thoughts of others – these may be helpful, but of far greater worth is to become someone who is familiar with the Word yourself, asking the Holy Spirit to speak to you through it and becoming adept at applying it to the circumstances of your life.

The Bible is a large book, and it can be very off-putting to start a journey of reading it through. But don't be hurried. You have the rest of your life to do this, so begin in manageable chunks. 5 minutes a day, 15 minutes a day, etc. Little and often (daily) is far better than to aim to do something extravagant, which is unsustainable for you. There are many apps and Bible reading plans online to help with this.

Whatever you choose, this MUST be an ongoing discipline in your life. Start with something and see where it leads you.

There is a tension that we navigate here, and it is this: when we first become Christians, we will obviously begin with an immaturity in the Word, but at the same time, we are indwelt by the Holy Spirit who comes in all His fullness and perfect wisdom. It is quite common for God to use other means to get our attention when we are new Christians, but as we mature guidance can become less dramatic. Over time we will gradually bridge this gap if we diligently become familiar with the Word.

In our experience, as this happens, we become more 'naturally discerning', and we become more able to apply the truth. We are never fully mature, and we will always be dependent on the Holy Spirit, but over time our interaction with the Word and with the Holy Spirit will deepen.

Serve. The journey of discovery is not just about us knowing more of who God is. It is also about giving space for God to show us more of who we are, how He has created us, and who we are in Christ. One of the best ways to find this out is to serve. Serve Him within the church context where you find yourself. If you want to find out whether you have a passion for children's work, then work with children. If you feel a burden to help drug addicts, then find a ministry that serves them. If you think you are a teacher, then find a way to share some of your thoughts – perhaps initially with one or two, or a small group. The church should be the best environment to recognise and affirm a call or gifting, but the only way we can know it is to begin to serve others.

Explore. The internet is full of many good resources that can be useful in exploring our personal gifting, and ministry opportunities. Be diligent in exploring these. As you do, do so with a simple prayer – 'Lord, lead me.' You may be very surprised what He shows you. Let it prompt conversations with others that you trust. Be vulnerable and share your findings with them. Ask them what they think. Ask them to pray with you, so that you can listen to God together. All this is part of learning to be a Body and not simply a collection of individuals.

A few final thoughts of reassurance…

During any journey of discernment, and over your whole life, God is sovereign. This is not merely a stated truth about who God is; this is an active reality for us to rest in. God speaks. That's what He does. He speaks in ways that we can understand, and at the perfect time. He can speak into our circumstances, whatever they may be.

However God speaks, and however He leads, the outcome should be marked with peace. The Hebrew concept of shalom implies a sense of wholeness, completeness, contentedness, and blessing. With this peace comes the conviction – This is the way (Isaiah 30:21).

Along with His peace and conviction should also come sufficient clarity and understanding about what to do next. This will act as a firm foundation for you to move forward in faith with a renewed assurance and confidence in God.

Norman Grubb was one of the early pioneers of WEC International. He had a wonderful prayer that encapsulates the type of relationship that we think is inspirational — '*Good morning Lord! What are you up to today? Can I be a part of it?*' You too can live this spontaneous, responsive life, grounded in a genuine desire and conviction that you'll do anything, and you'll go anywhere, because He loves you and you love Him.

So, understand you have the mind of Christ, develop the right heart and do the right things to prepare yourself for Him to speak and be alert to whatever He wants to say, however He chooses to say it. If you make this your 'way of life', you will find that your first steps, though perhaps small, will quickly lead to huge steps of faith. God is always looking for responsive people to participate in the things He is wanting to do.

CONCLUSION

'I am the good shepherd; I know my sheep and my sheep know me.'

John 10:14

Are you listening?

This is one of our favourite passages. Jesus speaks fondly of his 'sheep' – if you are a Christian, a follower of Jesus, that's you. He says that He knows us, and we know Him. He calls, we listen, and we follow. He is the good shepherd.

In modern times few of us live with any meaningful connection to the farming world, so it might be harder for us to connect with this story than for the original listeners. Today we see sheep in fields, and we might see shepherds herding sheep with dogs, skilfully guided by whistles and shouts to go exactly where the shepherd wants them to go; or with quad bikes if the terrain is large. Basically, the sheep are driven by a process of being 'pushed'.

This is not the idea behind the imagery that Jesus is using here. As we read the passage, we see something far richer and deeper.

In biblical times sheep were stored together in mixed flocks overnight, perhaps in a fenced area that could then easily be guarded against bears or whatever predators might fancy taking them. In the morning, the individual shepherds would open the gate and call them out. The sheep would recognise their own shepherd's voice and would then respond; when it wasn't their shepherd calling, they would remain. The shepherd would then walk off, calling, and his sheep would follow. They had grown accustomed to the voice and care of their shepherd – he was the source of all they needed: protection, food, water, care. He could be trusted and so they would follow.

In this image we see a better picture of what it means to walk with God. It's meant to be relational. We follow Him because He knows us, because He calls us and because we know His voice. He is the source of all we need in life. We trust, we listen, and we choose to follow, because we know that this is the best thing for us.

We believe that God is inviting us, you, couples, families, the family of God, teams, ministries, missions, and churches to walk in the garden with Him. He has many treasures to share with us as we journey together, and all the while He will be working out His glorious purposes to extend His Kingdom and build His Church.

Throughout the pages of scripture, we read of people who are in relationship with God, and who have a dialogue with Him. God speaks, people hear, and then they act. Down through Church history it seems clear to us that the people who have been most effective in the Kingdom have been those who listened, heard and responded to the voice of God. Indeed, the growth of the Kingdom seems synonymous with the obedience of God's people. The willingness of God's people to follow flows from a conviction about what they should be doing.

We wrote this book because we don't always see that within the Church today. But we think that this is what a normal life with God should look like. It is what we have been created, and redeemed, to experience. We see a connection between seeking, doing and fruitfulness. So, we are convinced that the more people seek the mind of God, the more fruit there will be in the church.

We live in an age where we want the quickest solution possible. Relationships don't beat to that rhythm. Intimacy, familiarity and depth come over time, with effort and commitment. So, we have not written this to offer a 'quick fix'. We are simply urging you to search hard for a treasure that is more satisfying and fulfilling then anything this world has to offer. Our hope is that more and more people will grow in their capacity to hear from God and be responsive to what He has to say. We long to see a renewed understanding of what it means to walk with God.

Our prayer is that, as capacity for discernment is developed, it will unleash creativity and diversity, conviction and engagement in the purposes of God.

So, what should you do now? Put this book on your shelf along with all the others? Please No!

The next step is to respond to His voice.

'Walk with Me' is the divine invitation set before you today.

ABOUT THE AUTHORS

By profession, John is qualified as a structural engineer and a secondary teacher, Pauline is qualified as a primary teacher. They have been married since 1990 and have four children and three grandsons. They have served together with WEC International as short-term, 1991-1993, and as long-term WEC members since 1999. During this time, they have worked in WEC's school for missionaries' children in Senegal, West Africa, and in various locations around the UK. For most of this time they have been involved in some form of leadership both in WEC and within a local Church context.

ABOUT SYNDO

Linking passion and purpose

SYNDO.co.uk

Are you wanting to discover God's purposes for your life, your Team, Church, Ministry or Mission?

Do you know what God has called you to but want someone to walk alongside as you make the transition or implement change?

Let us help you.

We provide a coaching service for Christians, churches, ministries and mission organisations/groups.

Our aim is to help you link your God-given passion with a purpose and strategy. This will lead to increased:

- commitment and engagement
- accountability and evaluation
- expectation and celebration

We believe that:

- discerning the purposes of God is a group process
- each member has a role to play
- the process is an important element of preparation
- ownership and participation are indicators of a successful process

If you believe you would benefit from this approach, or are interested in finding out more, then please contact us via the website or email: john.bagg@syndo.co.uk

Printed in Great Britain
by Amazon